THE COMPLETE
BRAIN
TRAINING
PUZZLES

— VOLUME I —

THIS IS A CARLTON BOOK

Published by Carlton Books Limited
20 Mortimer Street
London W1T 3JW

Copyright © 2009 Carlton Books Limited

ISBN 978-1-84732-462-7

Printed in China

THE COMPLETE
BRAIN
TRAINING
PUZZLES

VOLUME 1

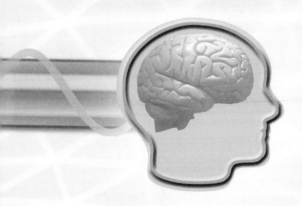

CARLTON
BOOKS

Introduction

Welcome to brain-training.

Perhaps your memory isn't what it used to be. Maybe you're here because you like puzzles. The good news – whatever your reason for picking up this book – is that solving puzzles is great brain exercise. Like your body, your brain needs some exercise to keep it healthy.

But looking after your brain isn't just a case of puzzling. Get enough sleep, avoid stress, exercise a bit, and watch what you eat. Strange advice from a puzzle book, but true none the less!

There are many different puzzle types in this book, and you can solve them in any order you choose. If you get stuck, just move on and come back to it later; you'll probably find it easy when you come back to it.

Don't give up, have fun, and above all enjoy!

Contents

Bits and Pieces

How can you mend a broken heart? Here's four you can practise on. Match each half heart with it's partner to make four whole ones.

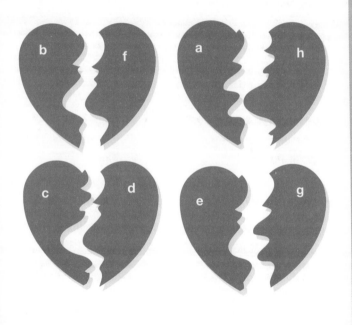

Answer on page 157

Boxes

Playing the game of boxes, each player takes it in turns to join two adjacent dots with a line. If a player's line completes a box, the player wins the box and has another go. It's your turn in the game below. To avoid giving your opponent a lot of boxes, what's your best move?

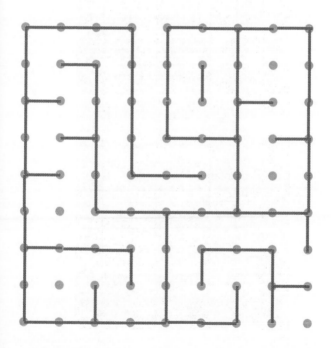

Answer on page 157

Colour Maze

Cross the maze from top to bottom. You may only pass from a green square to a red one, a red to a yellow, a yellow to a blue or a blue to a green, and you may not travel diagonally.

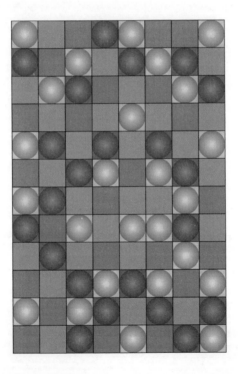

Answer on page 157

Cut and Fold

Which of the patterns below is created by this fold and cut?

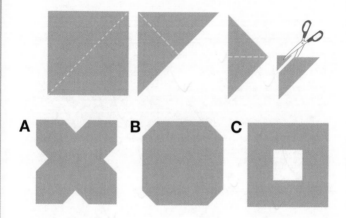

A

B

C

Answer on page 157

Double Drat

All these shapes appear twice in the box except one. Can you spot the singleton?

Answer on page 157

Game of Two Halves

Which two shapes below will pair up to create the top shape?

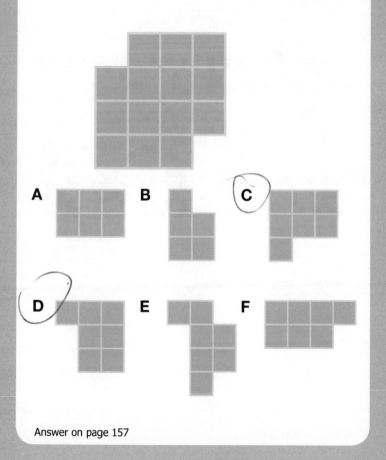

A **B** **C**

D **E** **F**

Answer on page 157

Get the Picture

These two grids, when merged together, wil make a picture...
Of what?

Answer on page 157

Gridlock

Which square correctly completes the grid?

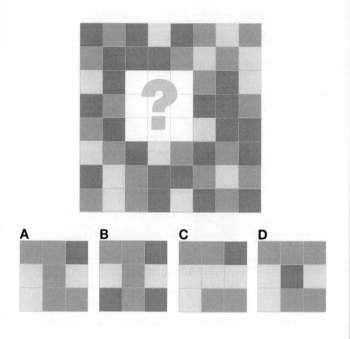

A   B   C   D

Answer on page 157

In the Area

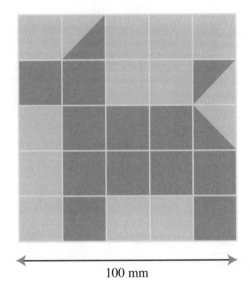

100 mm

Can you work out the approximate area that this dog is taking up?

Answer on page 158

Jigsaw

Which three of the pieces below can complete the jigsaw and make a perfect square?

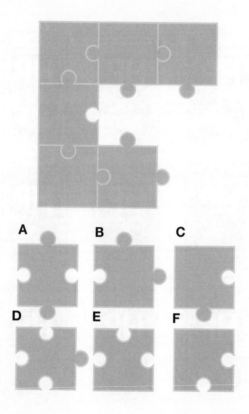

A

B

C

D

E

F

Answer on page 158

Where's the Pair?

Only two of these pictures are exactly the same. Can you spot the matching pair?

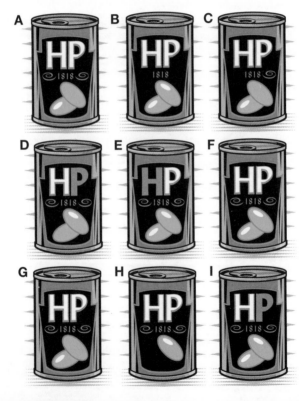

Answer on page 158

Symmetry

This picture, when finished, is symmetrical along a vertical line up the middle. Can you colour in the missing squares and work out what the picture is of?

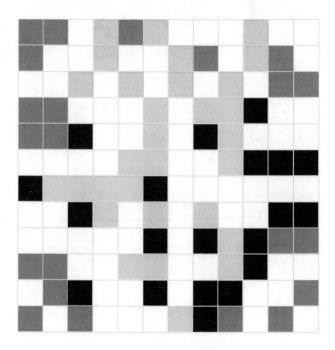

Answer on page 158

Sum People

Work out what number is represented by which person and replace the question mark.

4   11   ?

Answer on page 158

Spot the Difference

Can you spot ten differences between this pair of pictures?

Answer on page 158

Shape Shifting

Fill in the empty squares so that each row, column and long diagonal contains five different symbols

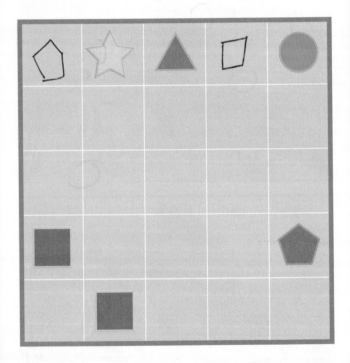

Answer on page 158

Scene It?

The four squares below can all be found in the picture grid – can you track them down? Beware, they may not be the right way up!

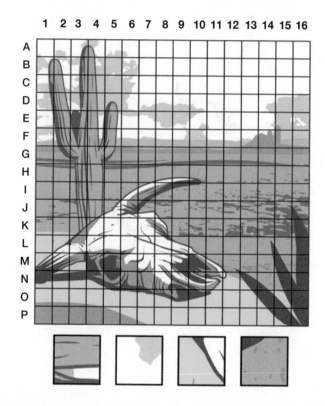

Answer on page 158

Rainbow Reckoning

This map can only be coloured in with three colours – blue, yellow and green. Assuming no two adjacent areas can be coloured the same, what colour will the area containing the question mark be?

Answer on page 159

Pots of Dots

How many dots should there be in the hole in his pattern?

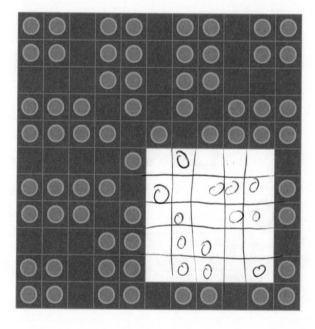

Answer on page 159

Picture Parts

Which box has exactly the right bits to make the pic?

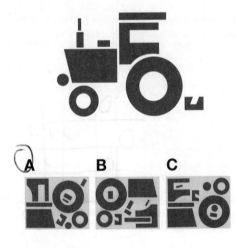

A **B** **C**

Answer on page 159

Odd Clocks

Buenos Aires is 11 hours behind Singapore, which is 7 hours ahead of London. It is 6.55 pm on Tuesday in London – what time is it in the other two cities?

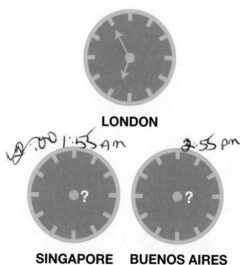

LONDON

12:00 1:55 Am   2:55 pm

SINGAPORE   **BUENOS AIRES**

Answer on page 159

Masyu

Draw a single continuous line around the grid that passes through all the circles. The line must enter and leave each box in the centre of one of its four sides.

Black Circle: Turn left or right in the box, and the line must pass straight through the next and previous boxes.

White Circle: Travel straight through the box, and the line must turn in the next and/or previous box.

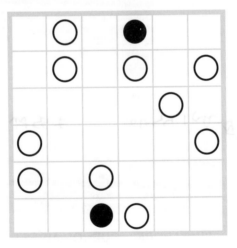

Answer on page 159

Matrix

Which of the boxed figures completes the set?

Answer on page 159

More or Less

The arrows indicate whether a number in a box is greater or smaller than an adjacent number. Complete the grid so that all rows and columns contain the numbers 1 to 5.

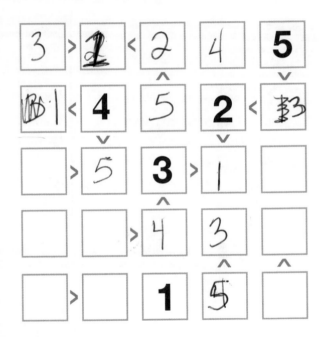

Answer on page 159

Paint by Numbers

Colour in the odd numbers to reveal... What?

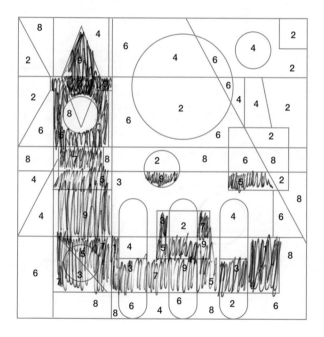

Answer on page 159

Face in the Crowd

Can you find one face in the crowd that isn't quite as happy as all the others?

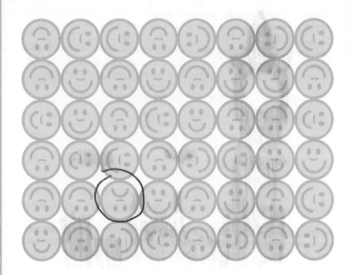

Answer on page 160

Piece Puzzle

Only one of these pieces fits the hole in our main
picture – the others have all been altered slightly by our artist.
Can you place the missing pic?

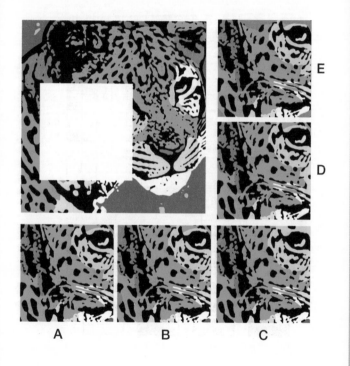

Answer on page 160

Scene It?

The four squares below can all be found in the picture grid, can you track them down? Beware, they may not be the right way up!

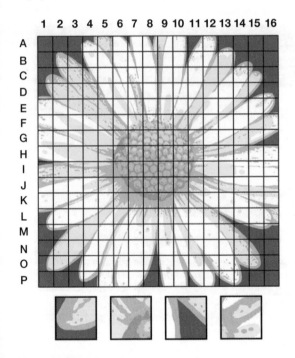

Answer on page 160

Spot the Difference

Can you spot ten differences between this pair of pictures?

Answer on page 160

Sudoku

Complete the grid so that all rows and columns, and each outlined block of nine squares, contain the numbers 1, 2, 3, 4, 5, 6, 7, 8 and 9.

8			1	7		2		
1		9			6		3	
	5			3	4		7	8
4			8	2		5	9	
	2		3		9		1	
	6							3
	4		7					2
		7		4	2	6	8	
	8		6		3		4	

Answer on page 160

Matrix

Which of the four boxed figures completes the set?

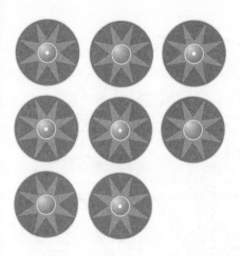

Answer on page 160

Riddle

An enclosure at the zoo contains both elephants and emus. If there are a total of 44 feet and 30 eyes, can you work out how many of each animal there is?

Answer on page 160

View From Above

Of the plan views below, only one of them is a true overhead representation of the scene shown here – can you work out which?

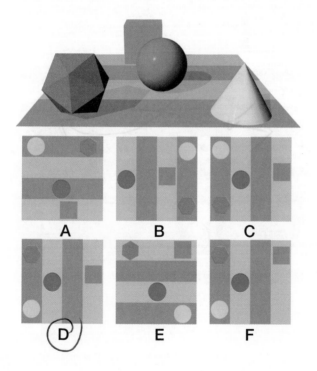

A

B

C

D

E

F

Answer on page 160

Bits and Pieces

Can you match the four broken tops of these vases with the bodies they belong to?

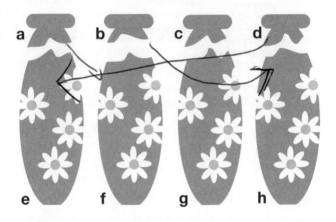

Answer on page 161

Cut and Fold

Which of the patterns below is created by this fold and cut?

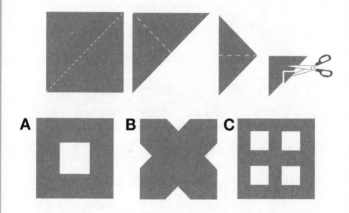

A

B

C

Answer on page 161

Location

Below is an altered view of a world famous landmark. Can you tell where it is?

Answer on page 161

Matrix

Which of the boxed figures completes the set?

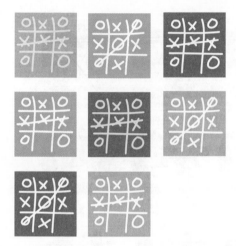 

Answer on page 161

Mirror Image

Only one of these pictures is an exact mirror image of the first one?
Can you spot it?

Answer on page 161

Number Jigsaw

The nine boxes that make up this grid can be rearranged to make a number. Which number?

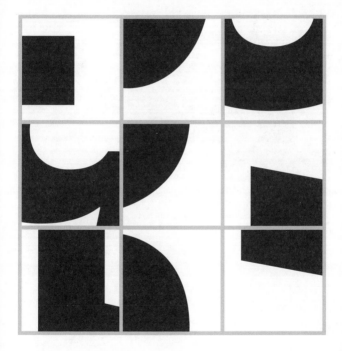

Answer on page 161

Patch of the Day

Place the shape in the grid so that no colour appears twice in the same row or column. Beware, the shape may not be the right way up!

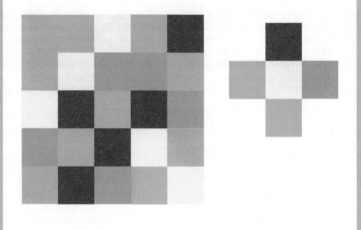

Answer on page 161

Pipes

Which two of the four boxes below can successfully fix the gaps in the pipes?

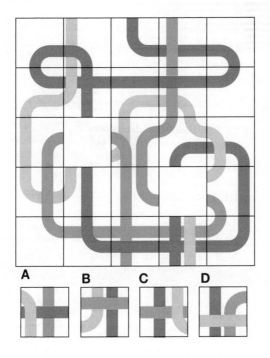

A   B   C   D

Answer on page 161

Missing Link

What should replace the red square with the question mark so that the grid follows a pattern?

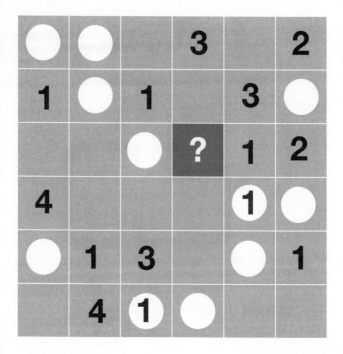

Answer on page 162

Picture Parts

Which box has exactly the right bits to make the pic?

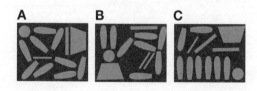

A

B

C

Answer on page 162

Scene It?

The four squares below can all be found in the picture grid – can you track them down? Beware, they may not be the right way up!

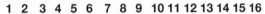

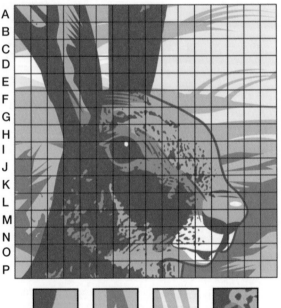

Answer on page 162

Sum People

Work out what number is represented by which person and replace
the question mark.

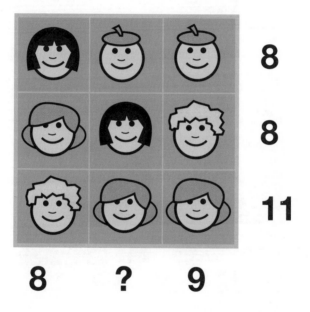

8 ? 9

Answer on page 162

Symmetry

This picture, when finished, is symmetrical along a vertical line up the middle. Can you colour in the missing squares and work out what the picture is of?

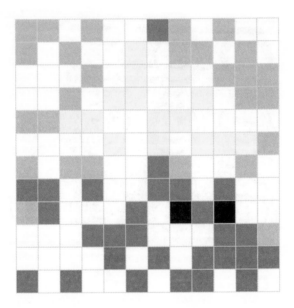

Answer on page 162

Usual Suspects

Officer Lassiter is having his new uniform and kit fitted. He has the helmet badge, but not the shoulder badges yet. He has his new radio, but hasn't yet received a new tie... Can you pick him out of the group?

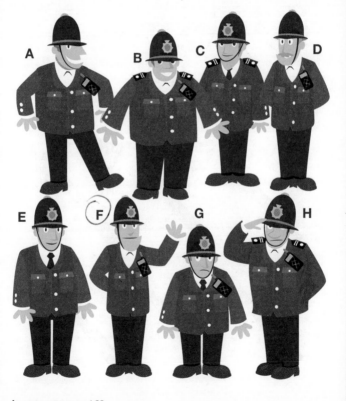

Answer on page 162

Where's the Pair?

Only two of these pictures are exactly the same. Can you spot the matching pair?

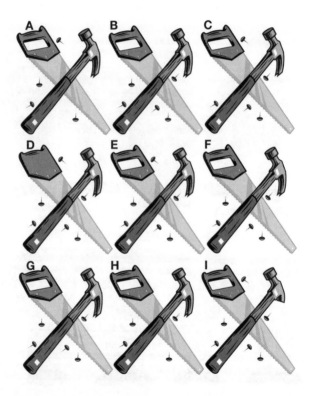

Answer on page 162

Which Wheel?

Which of the wheels, a, b, c, or d, is missing from the set below?

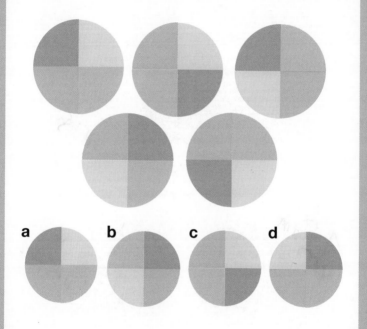

Answer on page 162

Odd Clocks

Madrid is 7 hours behind Tokyo, which is 1 hour behind Melbourne. It is 6.15 am on Saturday in Tokyo – What time is it in the other two cities?

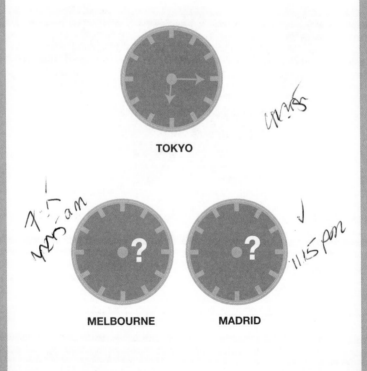

TOKYO

MELBOURNE

MADRID

Answer on page 163

Where's the Pair?

Only two of the shapes below are exactly the same – can you find the matching pair?

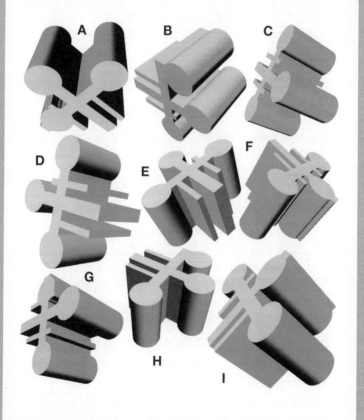

Answer on page 163

Where's the Pair

Only two of these pictures are exactly the same. Can you spot the matching pair?

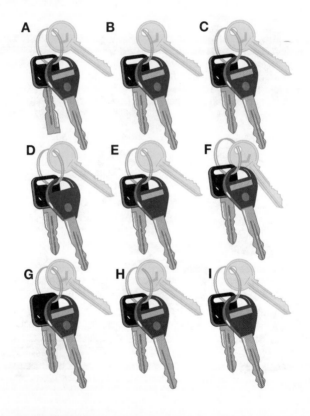

Answer on page 163

Usual Suspects

Banjo the clown has blue hair, but not a blue collar. He always wears a flower in his lapel and a comedy hat. Can you pick him out?

Answer on page 163

Sum Total

Replace the question marks with mathematical symbols (+, −, × or ÷) to make a working sum.

$$21 \; ? \; 3 \; ? \; 7 \; ? \; 1 = 8$$

Answer on page 163

Picture Parts

Which box has exactly the right bits to make the pic?

A   **B**   **C**

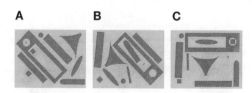

Answer on page 163

Magic Squares

Complete the square using nine consecutive numbers, so that all rows, columns and large diagonals add up to the same total.

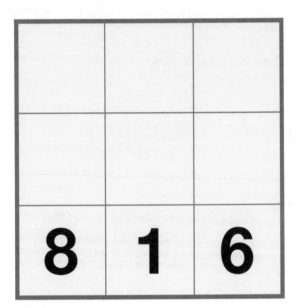

Answer on page 163

Deep Sea Dresser

Arrange this set of diver pics in the correct order from boxers to ocean- prepared.

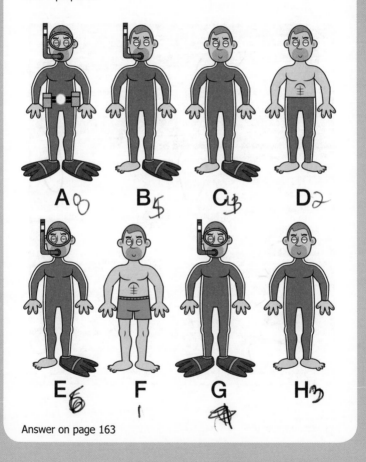

A 8   B 5   C 4   D 2

E 6   F 1   G 7   H 3

Answer on page 163

Can You Spot?

We've hidden ten spanners in this garage – Can you spot them all?

Answer on page 163

All Change

The colour of each triangle in pattern **B** is directly related to the colours in pattern **A**. Can you apply the same the rules and fill in pattern **C**?

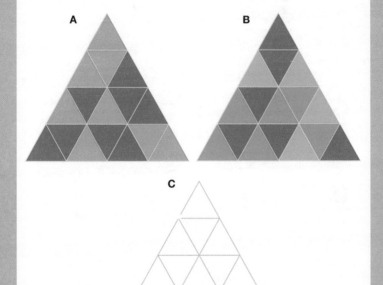

Answer on page 164

Game of Two Halves

Which two shapes below will pair up to create the top shape?

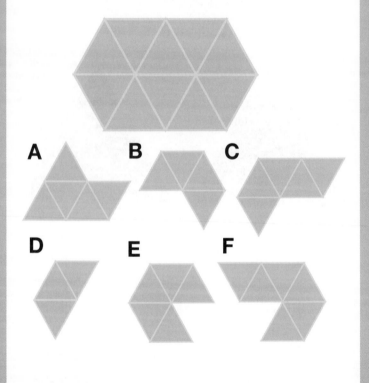

A

B

C

D

E

F

Answer on page 164

Hub Signs

What numbers should appear in the hubs of these number wheels?

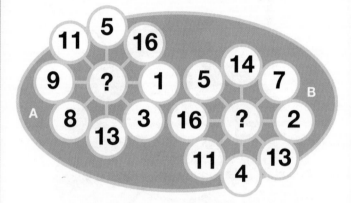

Answer on page 164

Riddle

Billy bought a bag of oranges on Monday and ate a third of them. On Tuesday he ate half of the oranges he had left. On Wednesday he found he had two oranges left. How many did he start with?

Answer on page 164

View From Above

Of the plan views below, only one of them is a true overhead representation of the scene shown here – can you work out which?

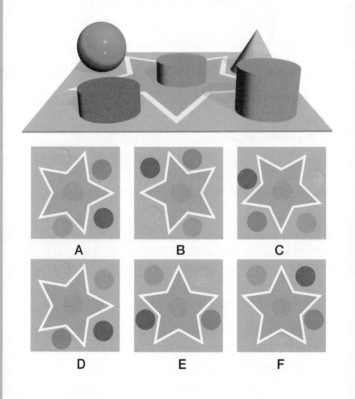

A

B

C

D

E

F

Answer on page 164

Cats and Cogs

Turn the handle in the indicated direction... Does the cat go up or down?

Answer on page 164

Checkers

Make a move for white so that eight black pieces are left, none of which are in the same column or row.

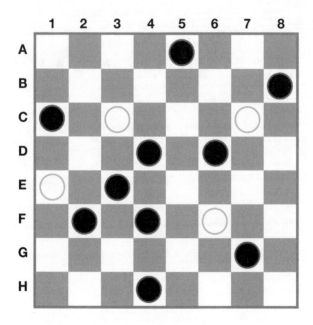

Answer on page 164

Get the Picture

These two grids, when merged together, will make a picture...
Of what?

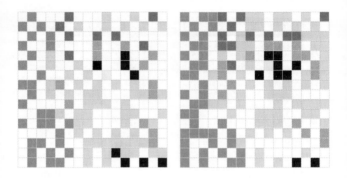

Answer on page 165

In the Area

Can you work out the approximate area this bird is taking up?

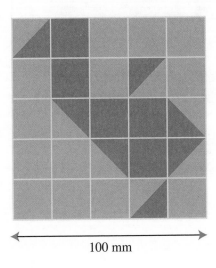

← 100 mm →

Answer on page 165

Matrix

Which of the boxed figures completes the set?

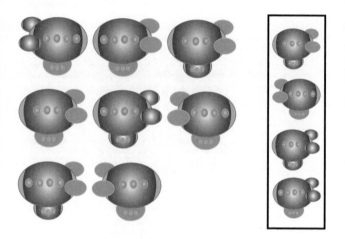

Answer on page 165

Missing Link

What should replace the square with the question mark so that the grid follows a pattern?

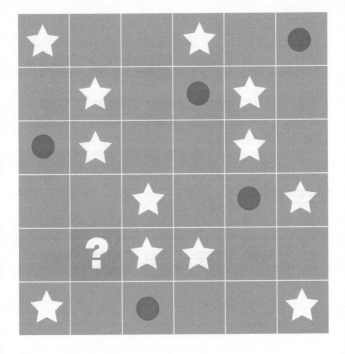

Answer on page 165

Symbol Sums

These symbols represent the numbers 1 to 4. If the green phone represents the number 3, can you work out what the other colour phones are representing and make a working sum?

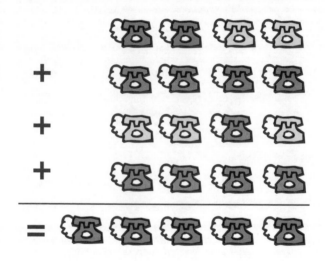

Answer on page 165

Symmetry

This picture, when finished, is symmetrical along a vertical line up the middle. Can you colour in the missing squares and work out what the picture is of?

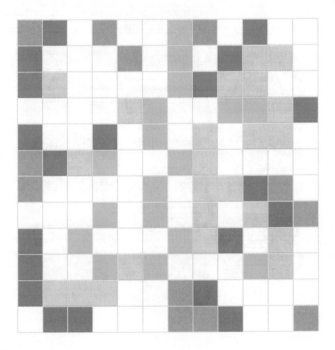

Answer on page 165

Where's the Pair?

Only two of these pictures are exactly the same. Can you spot the matching pair?

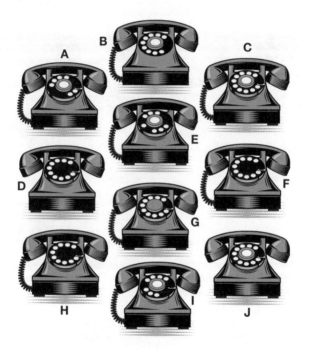

Answer on page 166

Sum Total

Replace the question marks with mathematical symbols (+,−, × or ÷) to make a working sum.

$$16 \; ? \; 2 \; ? \; 3 \; ? \; 1 = 6$$

Answer on page 166

Pool Puzzle

You're playing stripes in a game of pool, and you've cleaned up all your balls. Just the black remains. Can you spot the shot?

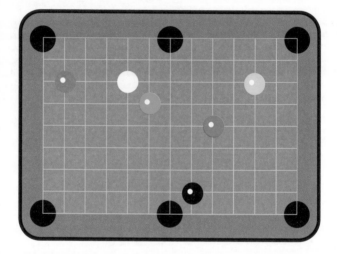

Answer on page 166

Piece Puzzle

Only one of these pieces fits the hole in our main picture – the others have all been altered slightly by our artist. Can you place the missing pic?

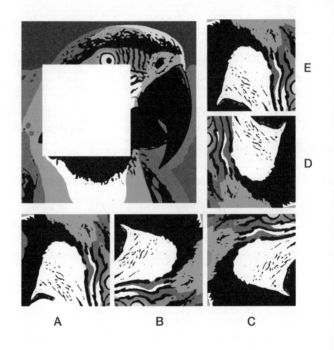

E

D

A

B

C

Answer on page 166

Patch of the Day

Place the shape over the grid so that no colour appears twice in the same row or column. Beware, the shape may not be the right way up!

Answer on page 166

More or Less

The arrows indicate whether a number in a box is greater or smaller than an adjacent number. Complete the grid so that all rows and columns contain the numbers 1 to 5.

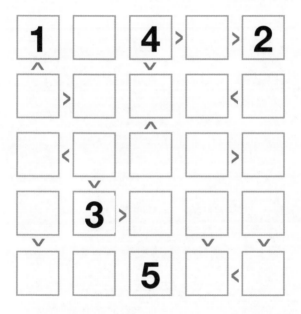

Answer on page 166

Riddle

It's night time in your bedroom and the light has broken. You're getting dressed and need a pair of socks. You've got 10 red, 8 white and 12 grey socks in a drawer – how many do you have to pull out in the dark before you know you have a matching pair?

Answer on page 166

All Change

The colour of each square in pattern B is directly related to the colours in pattern A. The square colours in pattern C relate to pattern B the same way. Can you apply the same the rules and fill in pattern D?

A

B

C

D

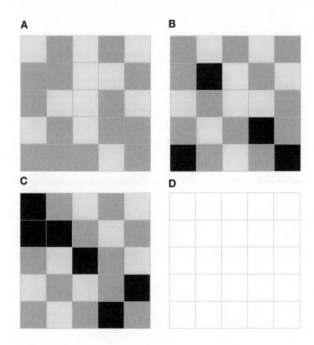

Answer on page 166

Boxes

Playing the game of boxes, each player takes it in turns to join two adjacent dots with a line. If a player's line completes a box, the player wins the box and has another go. It's your turn in the game below. To avoid giving your opponent a lot of boxes, what's your best move?

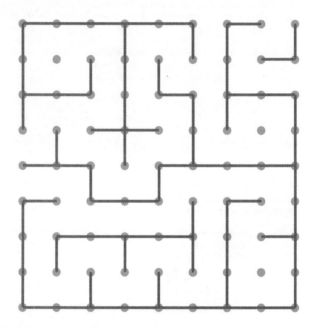

Answer on page 166

Double Drat

All these numbers appear twice in the box except one. Can you spot
the singleton?

Answer on page 166

Boats and Buoys

Every buoy 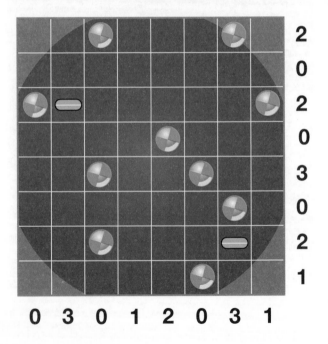 has one boat found horizontally or vertically adjacent to it. No boat can be in an adjacent square to another boat (even diagonally). The numbers by each row and column tell you how many boats are there. Can you locate all the boats?

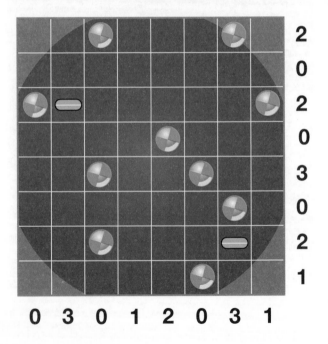

Answer on page 167

Riddle

Tony and Tina go shopping and on the way home Tina says, "Hey! If you gave me one of your bags, I'd have twice as many as you – but if I gave you one of mine, we'd have the same number!" Can you work out how many bags they have each?

Answer on page 167

Cubism

The shape below can be folded to make a cube. Which of the four cubes pictured below could it make?

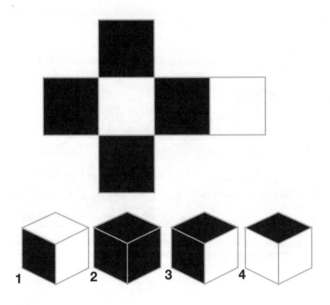

Answer on page 167

Cut and Fold

Which of the patterns below is created by this fold and cut?

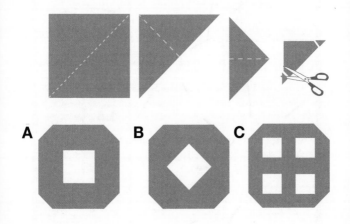

A

B

C

Answer on page 167

Latin Square

Complete the grid so that every row and column, and every outlined area, contains the letters A, B, C, D, E and F

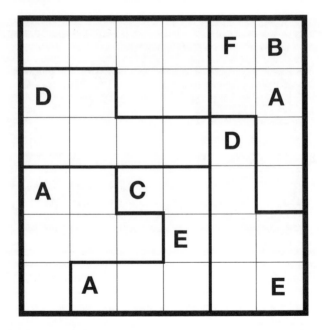

Answer on page 167

Location

Below is an altered view of a world-famous landmark. Can you tell where it is?

Answer on page 167

Masyu

Draw a single continuous line around the grid that passes through all the circles. The line must enter and leave each box in the centre of one of its four sides.

Black Circle: Turn left or right in the box, and the line must pass straight through the next and previous boxes.

White Circle: Travel straight through the box, and the line must turn in the next and/or previous box.

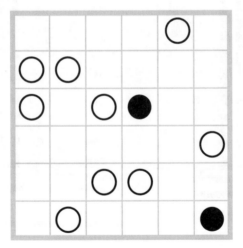

Answer on page 167

92

Matrix

Which of the boxed figures completes the set?

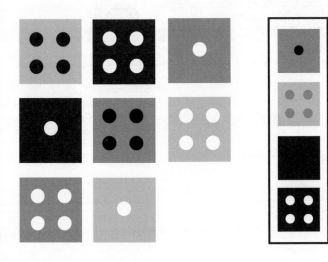

Answer on page 167

Next!

Which of the balls, A, B, C or D is the logical next step in this sequence?

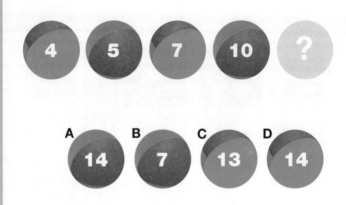

4   5   7   10   ?

A 14   B 7   C 13   D 14

Answer on page 168

Next!

Which of the balls, A, B, C or D is the logical next step in this sequence?

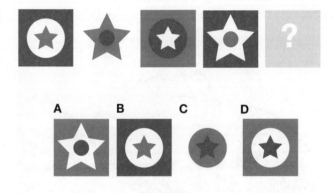

Answer on page 168

Riddle

A fish is 45 centimetres long, and its head is as long as its tail. If its head were twice as long as it really is, the head and tail together would be as long as the middle part of the fish. How long is each part of the fish?

Answer on page 168

Bits and Pieces

Can you match the four broken windows with the pieces of glass below?

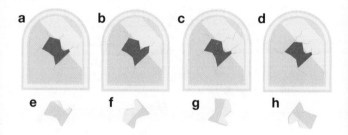

Answer on page 168

Block Party

Assuming all blocks that are not visible from this angle are present, how many blocks have been removed from this 6 × 6 × 6 cube?

Answer on page 168

Picture Parts

Which box has exactly the right bits to make the pic?

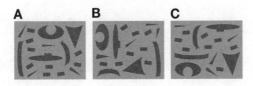

Answer on page 168

Pots of Dots

How many dots should there be in the hole in this pattern?

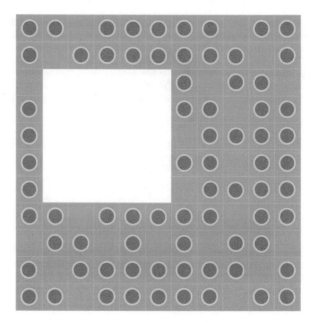

Answer on page 168

Get the Picture

These two grids, when merged together, will make a picture...
Of what?

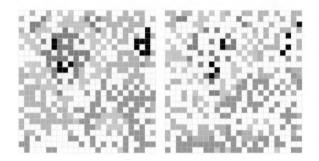

Answer on page 168

Rainbow Reckoning

This wall is to be painted in Green, Blue and Lilac, with no adjacent bricks to be in the same colour. Can you work out what colour the window frame should be?

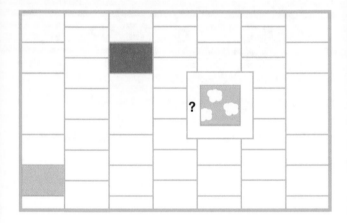

Answer on page 169

Sum Total

Replace the question marks with mathematical symbols (+, −, × or ÷) to make a working sum.

$$9 \ ? \ 2 \ ? \ 3 \ ? \ 9 = 6$$

Answer on page 169

Spot the Difference

Can you Spot ten Differences between this pair of pictures?

Answer on page 169

Symmetry

This picture, when finished, is symmetrical along a vertical line up the middle. Can you colour in the missing squares and work out what the picture is of?

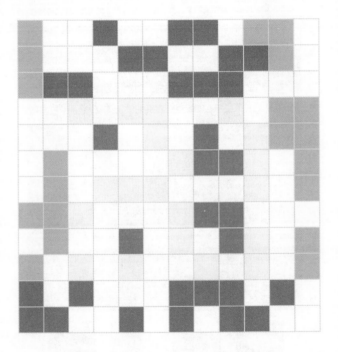

Answer on page 169

Scene It?

The four squares below can all be found in the picture grid – can you track them down? Beware, they may not be the right way up!

Answer on page 169

Riddle

You are in a room, blindfolded, with a bowl containing 50, 20, 10 and 5 dollar bills. You are allowed to take notes out of the bowl one at a time until you have four notes of the same value. What's the largest amount of cash you could end up with?

Answer on page 169

Block Party

Assuming all blocks that are not visible from this angle are present, how many blocks have been removed from this 5 × 5 × 5 cube?

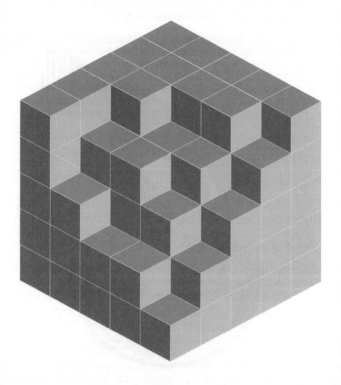

Answer on page 169

Boxes

In the game of boxes, each player takes it in turns to join two adjacent dots with a line. If a player's line completes a box, the player wins the box and has another go. It's your turn in the game below. Can you give your opponent just one box?

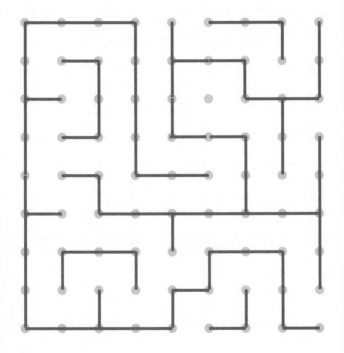

Answer on page 169

Boxes

In the game of boxes, each player takes it in turns to join two adjacent dots with a line. If a player's line completes a box, the player wins the box and has another go. It's your turn in the game below. Can you give your opponent just one box?

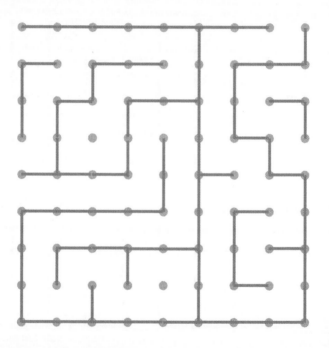

Answer on page 170

Checkers

Make a move for white so that eight black pieces are left, none of which are in the same column or row.

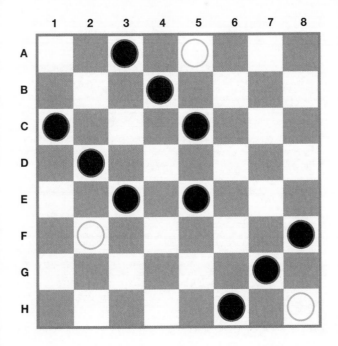

Answer on page 170

Double Drat

All these letters appear twice in the box except one. Can you spot the singleton?

Answer on page 170

Dressing Snowman

Arrange this set of snowman pics in the correct order from bare ball of snow to fully fledged.

Answer on page 170

Game of Two Halves

Which two shapes below will pair up to create the top shape?

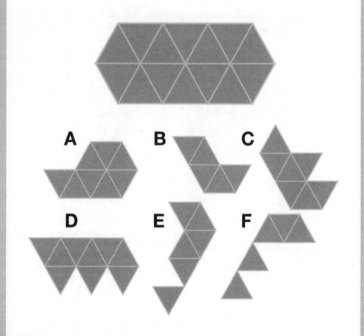

A

B

C

D

E

F

Answer on page 170

Get the Picture

These two grids, when merged together, will make a picture...
Of what?

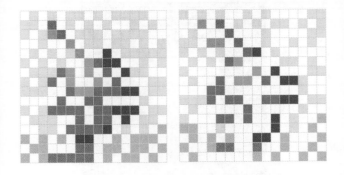

Answer on page 170

Gridlock

Which square correctly completes the grid?

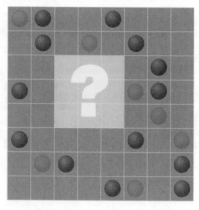

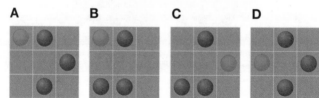

A   B   C   D

Answer on page 170

Riddle

Celebrity chef, Gordon Ramsfoot discovered one Sunday morning that his toaster had broken and he had three hungry kids on his hands. It takes exactly one minute to toast one side of a piece of bread using the grill, but the grill only takes two pieces of bread at a time. In a terrible hurry as always, can you work out how he managed to make three pieces of toast, using the grill, in just three minutes?

Answer on page 170

X and O

The numbers around the edge of the grid describe the number of X's in the vertical, horizontal and diagonal lines connecting with that square. Complete the grid so that there is an X or O in every square.

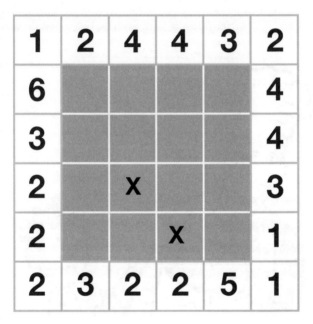

Answer on page 171

Gridlock

One of the squares below correctly replaces the question mark and completes the grid. Can you work out which?

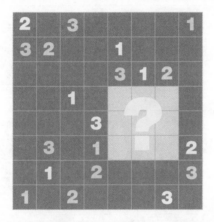

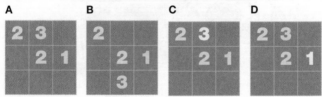

A   **B**   **C**   **D**

Answer on page 171

Where's the Pair?

Only two of these pictures are exactly the same. Can you spot the matching pair?

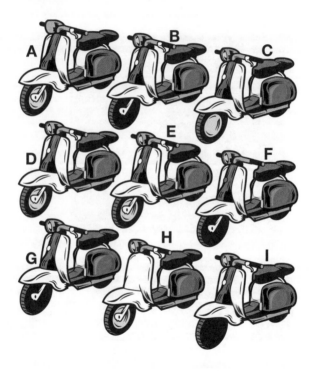

Answer on page 171

Hue Goes There

Three of the sections below can be found in our main grid, one cannot. Can you spot the section that doesn't belong? Beware, the sections might not be the same way round!

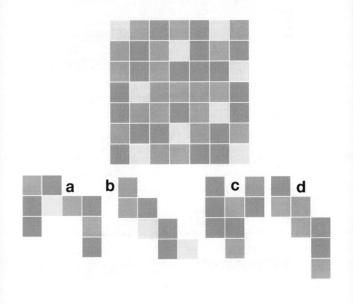

Answer on page 171

Usual Suspects

Flutter the fairy has a magic wand and wings, but she doesn't wear a crown and hasn't got a bow on her dress. Can you pick her out?

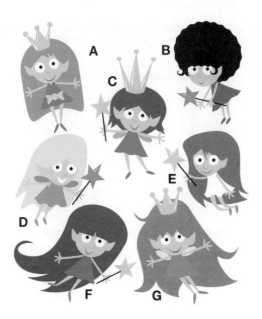

Answer on page 171

In the Area

Can you work out the approximate area this letter Q is taking up?

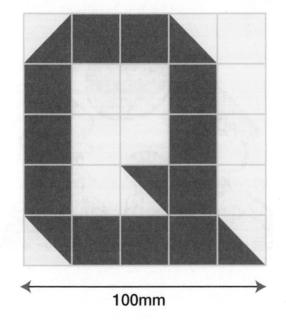

100mm

Answer on page 171

Think of a number

Officers Kaplutski and Wojowitz like a doughnut while they work. On a week long stakeout, Kaplutski ate 12 jam doughnuts and Wojowitz ate 28. What percentage of all the doughnuts eaten did Wojowitz account for?

Answer on page 171

Jigsaw

Which three of the pieces below can complete the jigsaw?

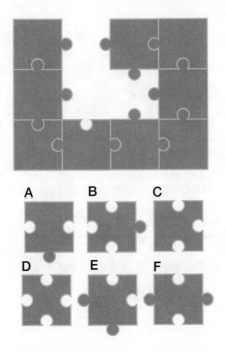

A   B   C

D   E   F

Answer on page 171

Symmetry

This picture, when finished, is symmetrical along a vertical line up the middle. Can you colour in the missing squares and work out what the picture is of?

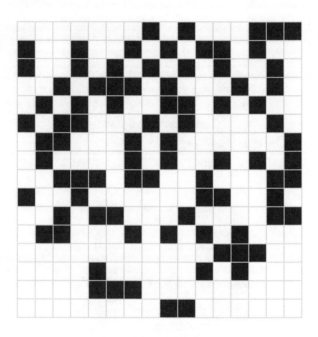

Answer on page 171

Logic Sequence

The dice below have been rearranged. Can you work out the new sequence from the clues given below?

The blue dice is between two odd numbers. The green dice is immediately to the left of the number 1. The number 2 is immediately to the right of the yellow dice. The two dice on the far left hand side add up to ten.

Answer on page 171

Matrix

Which of the boxed figures completes the set?

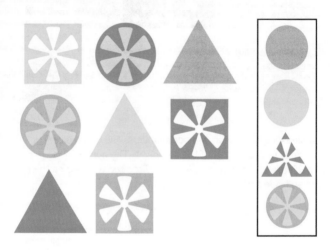

Answer on page 172

Matrix

Which of the boxed figures completes the set?

Answer on page 172

Matrix

Which of the boxed figures completes the set?

Answer on page 172

Mirror Image

Only one of these pictures is an exact mirror image of the first one? Can you spot it?

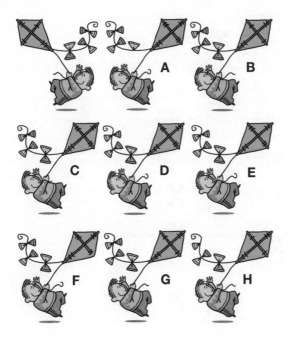

Answer on page 173

Missing Link

What should replace the square with the question mark so that the grid follows a pattern?

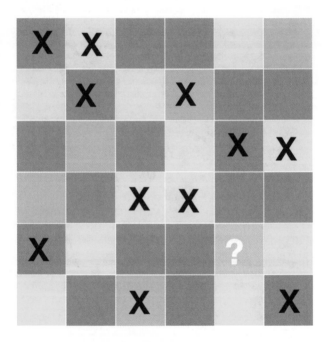

Answer on page 173

Next!

Which of the balls, A, B, C or D is the logical next step in his sequence?

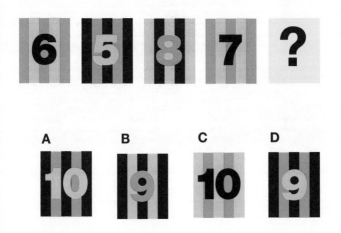

A   **B**   **C**   **D**

Answer on page 173

Number Mountain

Replace the question marks with numbers so that each pair of blocks adds up to the block directly above them.

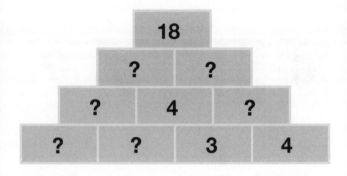

Answer on page 173

Odd Clocks

Paris is 2 hours behind Athens, which is 2 hours behind Karachi. It is 1.50 am on Sunday in Athens – what time is it in the other two cities?

ATHENS

KARACHI   **PARIS**

Answer on page 173

Paint by Numbers

Colour in the odd numbers to reveal... What?

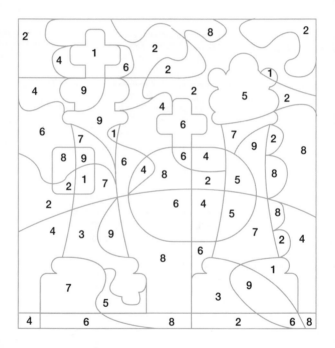

Answer on page 173

Picture Parts

Which box contains exactly the right bits to make the pic?

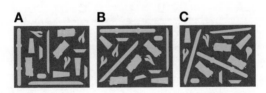

Answer on page 173

Picture Parts

Which box contains exactly the right bits to make the pic?

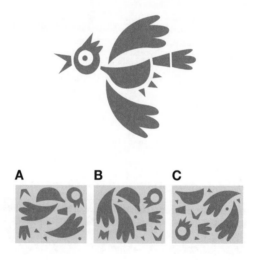

A   **B**   **C**

Answer on page 173

Piece Puzzle

Only one of these pieces fits the hole in our main picture - the others have all been altered slightly by our artist. Can you place the missing pic?

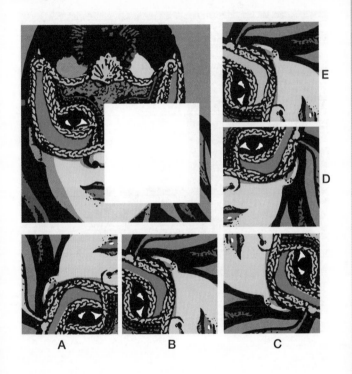

Answer on page 173

Pots of Dots

How many dots should there be in the hole in this pattern?

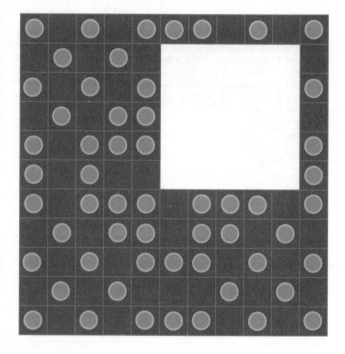

Answer on page 174

Rainbow Reckoning

This wall is to be painted in Green, Blue and Lilac, with no adjacent bricks to be in the same colour. Can you work out what colour the bottom right hand corner should be?

Answer on page 174

Reach for the Stars

Can you find three perfect five-pointed stars in this colourful collection?

Answer on page 174

Sum Total

Replace the question marks with mathematical symbols (+, −, × or ÷) to make a working sum.

$$4 \; ? \; 8 \; ? \; 7 \; ? \; 5 = 5$$

Answer on page 174

Scales

The arms of these scales are divided into sections – a weight two sections away from the middle will be twice as heavy as a weight one section away. Can you arranged the supplied weights in such a way as to balance the whole scale?

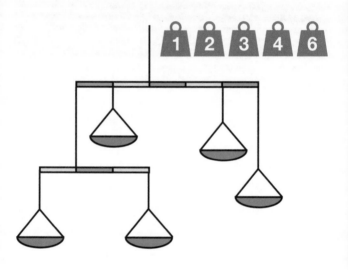

Answer on page 174

Sum People

Work out what number is represented by which person and replace the question mark.

15

8

14

11   15   ?

Answer on page 174

Scene It?

The four squares below can all be found in the picture grid – can you track them down? Beware, they may not be the right way up!

1 2 3 4 5 6 7 8 9 10 11 12 13 14 15 16

Answer on page 174

Sudoku Sixpack

Complete the grid so that every row, column and long diagonal contains the numbers 1, 2, 3, 4, 5 and 6

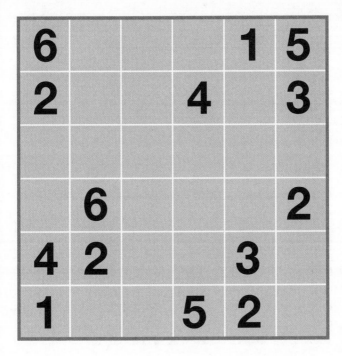

Answer on page 174

Shape Shifting

Fill in the empty squares so that each row, column and long diagonal contains five different symbols

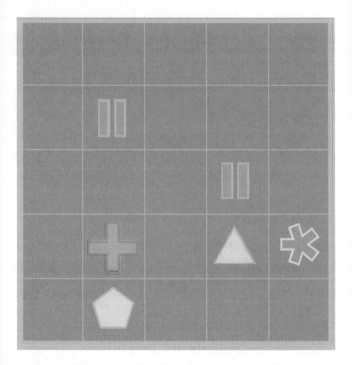

Answer on page 174

Spot the Difference

Can you spot ten differences between this pair of pictures?

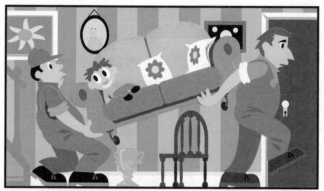

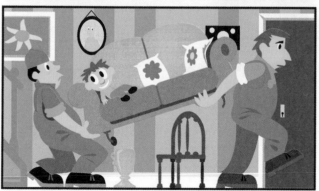

Answer on page 175

Shape Stacker

Can you work out the logic behind the numbers in these shapes, and suggest a number to replace the question mark?

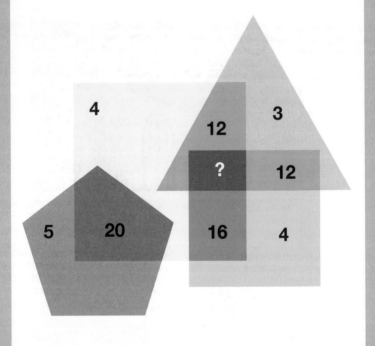

Answer on page 175

Shuffle

Fill in the grid so that each row, column and long diagonal contains four different shapes and the letters A, B, C and D

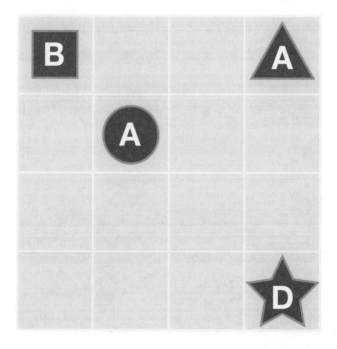

Answer on page 175

Shuffle

Fill in the shuffle box so that each row, column and long diagonal contains four different shapes and the letters A, B, C and D

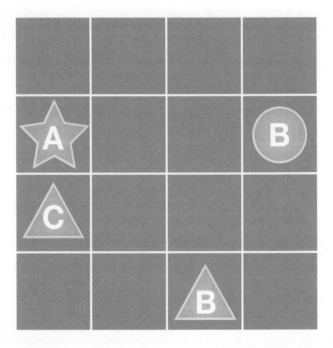

Answer on page 175

Signpost

Can you crack the logical secret behind the distances to these great cities, and work out how far it is to Karachi?

NEW YORK 11

OSLO 2

KARACHI ?

PARIS 5

GDANSK 13

Answer on page 175

Sum Total

Replace the question marks with mathematical symbols (+, −, × or ÷) to make a working sum.

35 ? 7 ? 4 ? 4 = 3

Answer on page 175

Riddle

In my shed at home I have some hamsters and some hamster cages. If I put one hamster in each cage I'd have one hamster too many. But if I put two hamsters in each cage, I'd have one cage left over... How many hamsters and cages have I got?

Answer on page 175

Piece Puzzle

Only one of these pieces fits the hole in our main picture – the others have all been altered slightly by our artist. Can you place the missing pic?

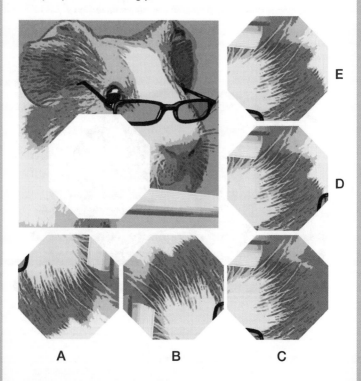

E

D

A

B

C

Answer on page 175

Answers

Page 6
Answer: A and G, B and D,
C and H, E and F

Page 7
Solution: A line on the right
or bottom of this square will
only give up one box to your
opponent

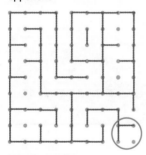

Page 8

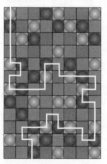

Page 9
Answer: A

Page 10

Page 11
Solution: C and D

Page 12
Solution below

Page 13
Answer: A. Each row and line in
the grid contains three green,
three red and two yellow squares

Answers

Page 14
Answer: 5,000 square millimetres.
Each 20 x 20 square represents
400mm². 12 and a half squares
are used

Page 15
Answer: A, C and E

Page 16
Answer: A and G are the pair.

Page 17
Solution below

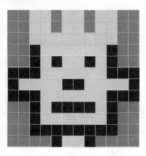

Page 18
Answer 6

1
2
3
4

Page 19

Page 20

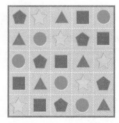

Page 21
Answer: F4, D14, L2, L15

Answers

Page 22
Answer: Yellow

Page 23
Solution: 13

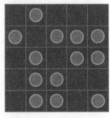

Page 24
Answer: A

Page 25
Answer: 1.55 am on Wednesday in Singapore and 2.55 pm on Tuesday in Buenos Aires

Page 26

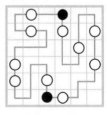

Page 27
Solution:

Each horizontal and vertical line contains a white star, a yellow star and a circled star. Each line contains a green and orange halved circle that has been turned through 0 degrees, 90 degrees and 180 degrees. The missing image should contain a white star, and a circle that has been turned through 90 degrees

3	1	2	4	5
1	4	5	2	3
5	2	3	1	4
2	5	4	3	1
4	3	1	5	2

Page 29
Solution: A Church

Answers

Page 30
Answer: The 5th face down in the third column

Page 31
Answer: A

Page 32
Answer: B2, G6, M2, G11

Page 33

Page 34

8	3	4	1	7	5	2	6	9
1	7	9	2	8	6	4	3	5
2	5	6	9	3	4	1	7	8
4	1	3	8	2	7	5	9	6
7	2	5	3	6	9	8	1	4
9	6	8	4	5	1	7	2	3
6	4	1	7	9	8	3	5	2
3	9	7	5	4	2	6	8	1
5	8	2	6	1	3	9	4	7

Page 35
Solution

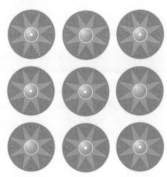

Each vertical and horizontal line contains one shape with all green triangles, one with all pink triangles and one with half pink and half green triangles. Each line also contains two shapes with a white dot in the centre and one with no white dot. The missing shape must have all green triangles and a white dot.

Page 36
Answer: 7 elephants and 8 emus

Page 37
Answer: D

Answers

Page 38
Answer: A and F, B and H,
C and E, D and G

Page 39
Answer: C

Page 40
Answer: The Leaning Tower
of Pisa

Page 41
Solution: Each horizontal
amd vertical line contains two
games where X's win, and
one where O's win. Each line
contains a green, an orange
and a blue square. Each line
contains two white games and
a yellow game. The missing
picture should be of a yellow
game on a green square
where X's win.

Page 42
Answer: D

Page 43

Page 44

Page 45
Answer: A and B

Answers

Page 46
Answer: A blue square containing a white circle and a black number 2. Each row and column contains two white circles and numbers that add up to five

Page 47
Answer: A

Page 48
Answer: M13, J16, A13, N7

Page 49
Solution: 10

1   2   3   5

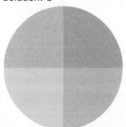

Page 50
Solution below

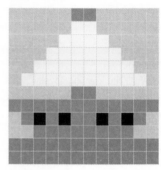

Page 51
Answer: Officer Lassiter is policeman F

Page 52
Answer: F and G are the pair.

Page 53
Solution: b

Answers

Page 54
Answer: 7.15 am on Saturday
in Melbourne
11.15 pm on Friday in Madrid

Page 55
Answer: D and E are the pair

Page 56
Answer: E and I are the pair

Page 57
Answer: Banjo is clown C

Page 58
Solution: $21 \times 3 \div 7 - 1 = 8$

Page 59
Answer: C

Page 60

Solution

4	9	2
3	5	7
8	1	6

Page 61
Answer: F, D, H, C, B, E, G, A

Page 62

Answers

Page 63

Answer: If its bordering triangles are predominantly orange, a triangle becomes red. If they are predominantly red, it becomes orange. If the bordering cells are equal in number, the triangle becomes pink, and if the bordering triangles have now become predominantly pink, it also becomes pink

Page 64
Solution: B and F

Page 65
Answer:
A) 8 – subtract the numbers opposite each other
B) 18 – Add the opposite numbers

Page 66
Answer: Six. He ate two on Monday and two more on Tuesday.

Page 67
Answer: D

Page 68
Answer: Down

Page 69

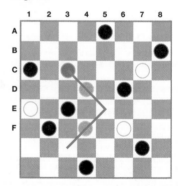

Answers

Page 70
Solution below

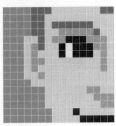

Page 71
Answer: 3400 square millimetres.
Each 20 x 20 square represents
400 mm². 5 squares (2000 mm²)
and 7 half-square triangles
(1400 mm²) form the bird

Page 72
Answer: Each horizontal and
vertical line contains two
airships with green fins, and
one with silvery fins. Each
line contains two airships with
green gondolas underneath,
and one with a silvery
gondola. Each line contains
two airships facing left and
one facing right. Each line
contains two airships with
four lights on the balloon, and
one with three lights.

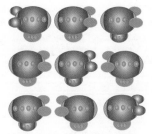

The missing image has silvery
fins, a green gondola, faces left
and has four lights on the balloon

Page 73
Answer: A green square
containing a red dot. All the rows
and columns should contain two
white stars and one red dot

Page 74
Solution
red 1   blue 2
green 3   yellow 4

Page 75
Solution below

Answers

Page 76
Answer: F and H are the pair

Page 77
Solution: $16 + 2 \div 3 \times 1 = 6$

Page 78

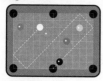

Page 79
Answer: B

Page 80

Page 81

Page 82
Answer: Just 4.

Page 83
Solution: If its bordering squares (not diagonals) are predominantly green, a square becomes green. If

they are predominantly yellow, it becomes yellow. If the bordering cells are equal In number, the square becomes black, and if the bordering squares have now become predominantly black, it also becomes black

Page 84
Solution: A line on the top or bottom of this square will only give up one box to your opponent

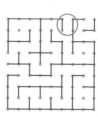

Page 85
Answer: 19

Answers

Page 86

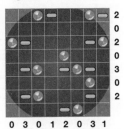

Page 87
Answer: Tony has 5 bags, Tina has 7

Page 88
Answer: 3

Page 89
Answer: B

Page 90

E	D	A	C	F	B
D	C	F	B	E	A
B	F	E	A	D	C
A	E	C	F	B	D
C	B	D	E	A	F
F	A	B	D	C	E

Page 91
Answer: The Statue of Liberty

Page 92

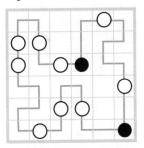

Page 93
Solution: Eachhorizontal or vertical line contains a group of 4 black dots, a group of 4 white dots and a single white dot. Each line contains a light blue symbol, a dark blue symbol and a black symbol. The missing picture must be a black symbol with 4 black (and therefore invisible) dots

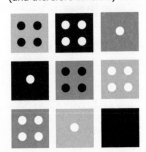

Answers

Page 94
Answer: D. The colours on the ball are alternating, while the number on it is increasing, by 1, then 2, then 3 etc

Page 95
Answer: D. The star and circle are swapping places each time. The smallest shape is taking the colour of the previous background square. The background square is taking the colour of the previous medium-sized shape, and the medium-sized shape is taking the colour of the previous smallest shape

Page 96
Answer: The head and tail are 9 centimetres long, the middle is 27 centimetres long

Page 97
Answer: A and G, B and H, C and F, D and E

Page 98
Answer: 76

Page 99
Answer: C

Page 100
Solution: 18

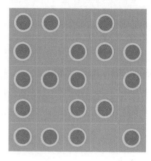

Page 101

Answers

Page 102
Answer: Lilac

Page 103
Solution: $9 \times 2 \times 3 \div 9 = 6$

Page 104

Page 105
Answer: M14, M2, F9, A4

Page 106
Solution below

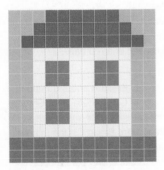

Page 107
Answer: $305 dollars. Three of each denomination and one more $50 bill

Page 108
Answer: 24

Page 109
Solution: A line on either side of this square will only give up one box to your opponent

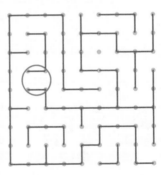

Answers

Page 110
Solution: A line on either side of this square will only give up one box to your opponent

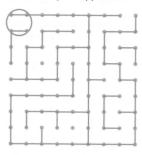

Page 111

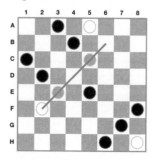

Page 112
Answer: A

Page 113
Answer: G, B, F, E, D, H, A, C

Page 114
Solution: D and F

Page 115
Solution below

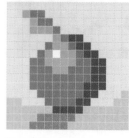

Page 116
Answer: B. Each row and line in the grid should contain two blue balls and one red ball

Page 117
Answer: Bread A and B go under the grill. One minute later, Gordon tuns bread A over and swaps bread B for Bread C. One minute later he removes bread A, turns over bread C and puts B back under for a further minute

Answers

Page 118

1	2	4	4	3	2
6	X	O	X	X	4
3	X	O	O	X	4
2	O	X	O	O	3
2	O	O	X	O	1
2	3	2	2	5	1

Page 119
Answer: A. Each row and column in the grid should contain the letters A, b and C, and one each of letters coloured yellow, blue and pink

Page 120
Answer: B and G are the pair

Page 121
Answer: b is the odd shape out

Page 122
Answer: Flutter is fairy D

Page 123
Answer: 5400 square millimetres. Each 20 × 20 square represents 400mm². 11 squares (4400mm²) and 5 half-square triangles (1000mm²) form the Q

Page 124
Answer: 70 percent. Total number of doughnuts - 40, becomes 100 when multiplied by 2.5. Multiply the other numbers by 2.5 to get percentages

Page 125
Answer: B, C and F

Page 126
Solution below

Page 127

Answers

Page 128

Solution: Each horizontal and vertical line contains 1 circle, 1 square and 1 triangle. Each line contains a yellow star, a white star and one picture without a star. Each line contains an orange symbol, a red symbol and a yellow symbol. The missing picture must be a yellow circle containing a yellow star

Page 129

Solution: Each horizontal and vertical line contains two green frames and a pink frame. Each horizontal and vertical line contains two green crosses and a pink cross. Each line contains a purple circle, a pink circle and no circle. The missing picture must be a green frame, with a pink cross and a pink circle

Page 130

Solution: Each horizontal and vertical line contains two black moustaches and a brown moustache. Each line contains one wink, and one tongue. Each line contains a yellow hat, a brown hat and a black hat. The missing picture must have a brown moustache, no wink, no tongue and a brown hat

Answers

Page 131
Answer: B

Page 132
Answer: A blue square
containing a cross. All the rows
and columns should contain
two crosses, three brown
squares, two yellow squares
and one blue square

Page 133
Answer: A. The numbers
are following a pattern of
minus 1, plus 3. The number
is taking the colour of the
old inside stripes, the inside
stripes are taking the colour
of the old outside stripes and
the outside stripes are taking
the colour of the old number

Page 134

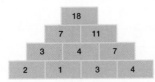

Page 135
Answer: 3.30am on Sunday in
Karachi, 11.90pm on Saturday in
Paris

Page 136
Solution: 2 Chess pieces

Page 137
Answer: B

Page 138
Answer: A

Page 139
Answer: B

Answers

Page 140
Solution: 12

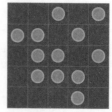

Page 141
Answer: Green

Page 142

Page 143
Solution: $4 \times 8 - 7 \div 5 = 5$

Page 144

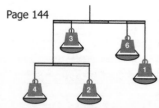

Page 145
Solution: 11

1

3

4

7

Page 146
Answer: E3, C9, D16, I6

Page 147

6	4	3	2	1	5
2	5	1	4	6	3
5	1	2	3	4	6
3	6	4	1	5	2
4	2	5	6	3	1
1	3	6	5	2	4

Page 148

Answers

Page 149

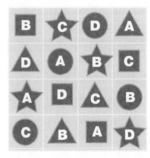

Page 150
Answer: 48.
The numbers represent the number of sides in the shape they occupy. when shapes overlap, the numbers are multiplied. $3 \times 4 \times 4 = 48$

Page 151

Page 152
Solution: 146

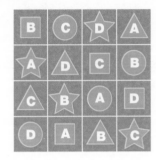

Page 153
Answer: 6. Score three for each consonant and two for a vowel. Subtract the vowel total from the consonant total. $12 - 6 = 6$

Page 154
Solution: $35 - 7 \div 4 - 4 = 3$

Page 155
Answer: 4 hamsters and 3 cages

Page 156
Answer: E

Intermediate Puzzles

Piece Puzzle

Only one of these pieces fits the hole in our main picture – the others have all been altered slightly by our artist. Can you place the missing pic?

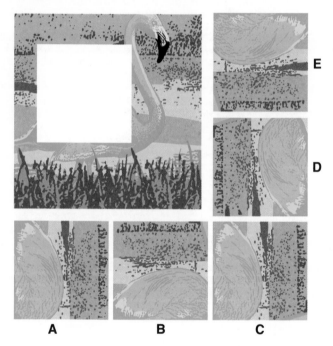

A   B   C

Answer on page 328

Boxes

Playing the game of boxes, each player takes it in turns to join two adjacent dots with a line. If a player's line completes a box, the player wins the box and has another go. It's your turn in the game below. To avoid giving your opponent a lot of boxes, what's your best move?

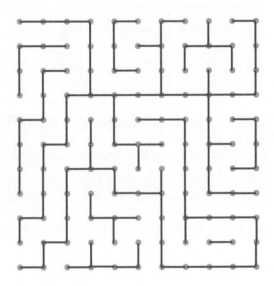

Answer on page 328

Cut and Fold

Which of the patterns below is created by this fold and cut?

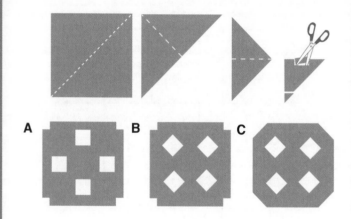

A   **B**   **C**

Answer on page 328

Dice Maze

On these dice each colour represents a direction – up, down, left and right. Starting in the middle die of the grid, follow the instructions correctly and you will visit every die in turn once only. What's the last die you visit on your trip?

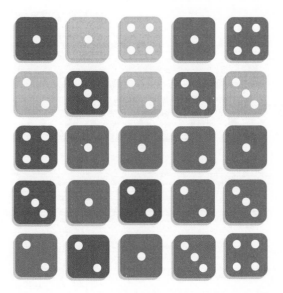

Answer on page 328

Follow That

The sequence below follows a logical pattern. Can you work out the number and colour next in line?

1 2 1 2 1 1 1 **?**

Answer on page 328

Magic Squares

Complete the square using nine consecutive numbers, so that all rows, columns and large diagonals add up to the same total.

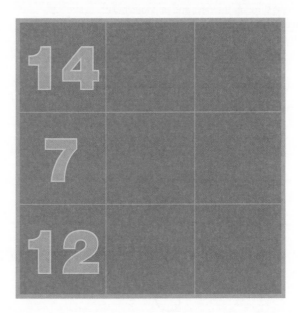

Answer on page 328

Masyu

Draw a single unbroken line around the grid that passes through all the circles. The line must enter and leave each box in the centre of one of its four sides.

Black Circle: Turn left or right in the box, and the line must pass straight through the next and previous boxes.

White Circle: Travel straight through the box, and the line must turn in the next and/or previous box.

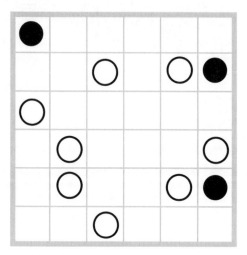

Answer on page 328

Matrix

Which of the four boxed figures completes the set?

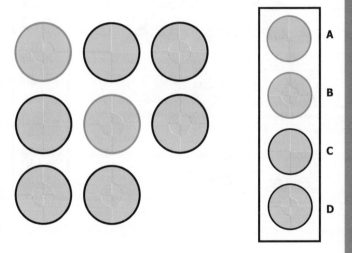

Answer on page 329

Matrix

Which of the boxed figures completes the set?

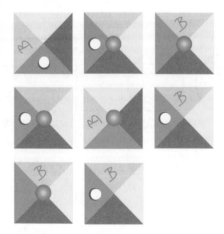 

Answer on page 329

Odd One Out

Which of the shapes below is not the same as the other ones?

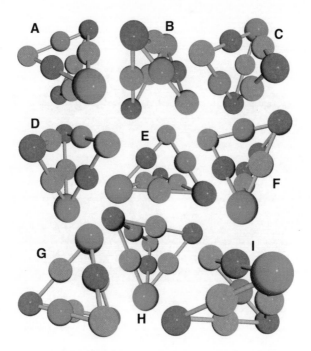

Answer on page 329

Riddle

Kitty has fallen down a well 12 metres deep. He can jump 3 metres up. But slides back 2 metres every time he lands. How many jumps gets kitty out of the well?

Answer on page 330

Scene It?

The four squares below can all be found in the picture grid – can you track them down? Beware, they may not be the right way up!

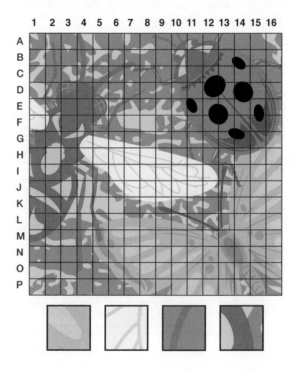

Answer on page 330

Think of a number

At the Sea View Guest house in Bournemouth, England over the course of one week they served 351 glasses of fruit juice with breakfast. 203 of them were orange, 31 were grapefruit, 39 were mango and 78 were apple. Can you work out what proportion of guests had citrus or non-citrus juices?

Answer on page 330

Weigh to Go

The coloured balls represent the numbers 1, 2, 3, 4 and 5. Can you work out which is which, and therefore how many yellow balls are required to balance the final scale?

Answer on page 330

Sudoku

Complete the grid so that all rows and columns, and each outlined block of nine squares, contain the numbers 1, 2, 3, 4, 5, 6, 7, 8 and 9.

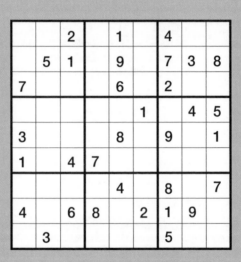

Answer on page 330

Sum People

Work out what number is represented by which person and fill in the question mark.

Answer on page 330

Tents and Trees

Every tree ▲ has one tent ▲ found horizontally or vertically adjacent to it. No tent can be in an adjacent square to another tent (even diagonally!). The numbers by each row and column tell you how many tents are there. Can you locate all the tents?

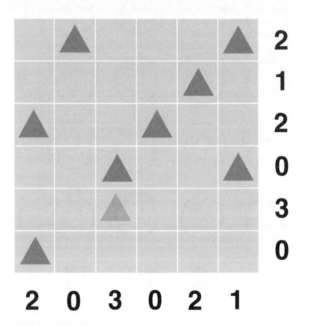

Answer on page 330

194

Signpost

Can you crack the logical secret behind the distances to these great cities, and work out how far it is to Washington?

BERLIN 16

CARDIFF 20

WASHINGTON ?

AUCKLAND 15

BEIJING 12

Answer on page 331

View from Above

Of the plan views below, only one of them is a true overhead representation of the scene shown here – can you work out which?

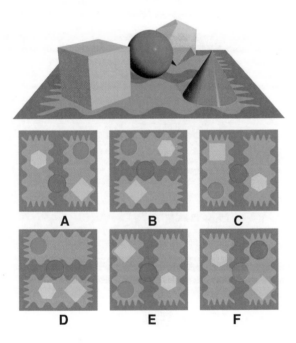

A

B

C

D

E

F

Answer on page 331

Block Party

Assuming all blocks that are not visible from this angle are present,
how many blocks have been removed from this 6 x 6 x 6 cube?

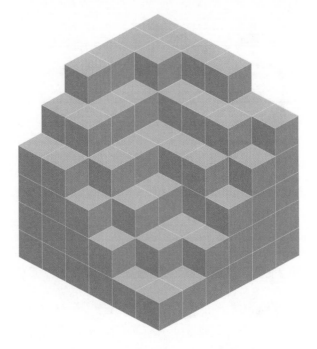

Answer on page 331

Where's the Pair

Only two of the shapes below are exactly the same – can you find the matching pair?

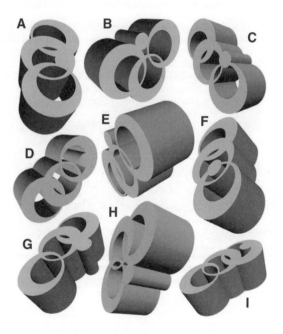

Answer on page 331

Colour Maze

Find the path from one white square to the other. You may only pass from a blue square to a red one, a red to a yellow, a yellow to a purple or a purple to a blue, and you may not travel diagonally.

Answer on page 331

Cube Route

Can you crack the colour code and make your way from one yellow square to the other? The blue arrow tells you which way is up...

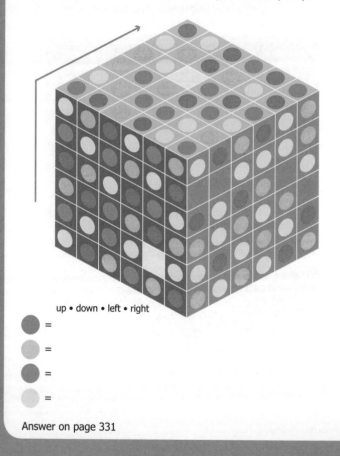

up • down • left • right

● =

● =

● =

● =

Answer on page 331

Double Drat

All these shapes appear twice in the box except one. Can you spot the singleton?

Answer on page 331

Get the picture

These two grids, when merged together, will make a picture...
Of what?

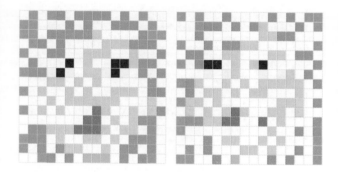

Answer on page 331

Hue Goes There

Three of the sections below can be found in our main grid, one cannot. Can you spot the section that doesn't belong? Beware, the sections might not be the same way round!

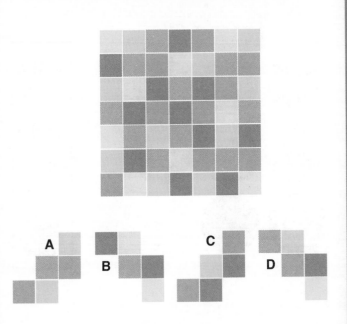

A

B

C

D

Answer on page 332

Matrix

Which of the boxed figures completes the set?

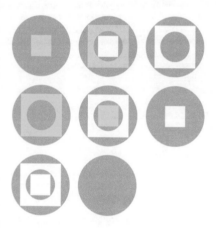 

Answer on page 332

Mini Nonogram

The numbers by each row and column describe black squares and groups of black squares that are adjoining. Colour in all the black squares and a six number combination will be revealed.

					1										
				1	1										
				1	1				5				1		
				1	1				1			3	1		
				3	1	5		3	1			1	1	5	
				1	1	5		1	1	5		3	1	5	

			3	1	3
		1	1	1	1
			3	1	3
			1	1	1
			3	1	3
		3	3	1	1
1	1	1	1	1	1
			3	3	3
			1	1	1
			3	3	1

Answer on page 332

More or Less

The arrows indicate whether a number in a box is greater or smaller than an adjacent number. Complete the grid so that all rows and columns contain the numbers 1 to 5.

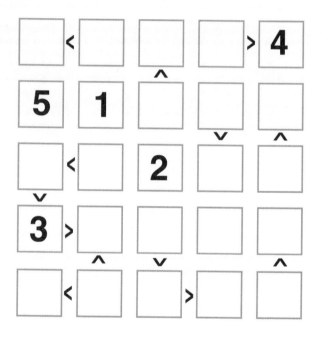

Answer on page 332

Patch of the Day

Place the shape over the grid so that no colour appears twice in the same row or column. Beware, the shape may not be the right way up!

Answer on page 332

Percentage Point

What percentage of this grid is blue and what percentage is yellow?

Answer on page 332

Riddle

Lucy met a pig and a goat in the woods and asked them what day it was, knowing full well that pigs always tell lies on Mondays, Tuesdays and Wednesdays, and that goats always tell lies on Thursdays, Fridays and Saturdays. She asked the pig first. 'Well, yesterday was one of my lying days', he said. She asked the goat. 'Yesterday was one of my lying days too', he said... So what day is it?

Answer on page 332

Scene It?

The four squares below can all be found in the picture grid – can you track them down? Beware, they may not be the right way up!

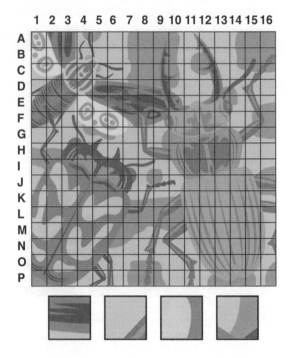

Answer on page 333

Symmetry

This picture, when finished, is symmetrical along a vertical line up the middle. Can you colour in the missing squares and work out what the picture is of?

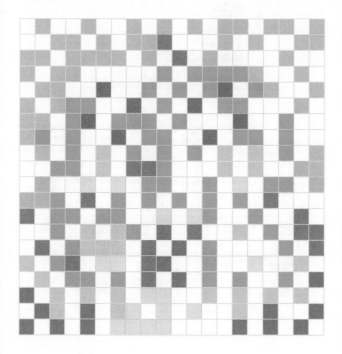

Answer on page 333

View from Above

Of the plan views below, only one of them is a true overhead representation of the scene shown here – can you work out which?

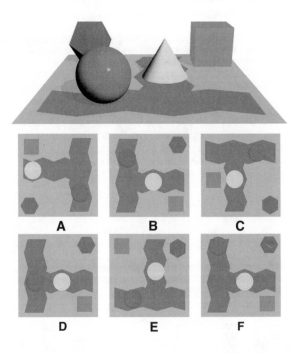

A

B

C

D

E

F

Answer on page 333

Box It

The value of each shape is the number of sides each shape has, multiplied by the number within it. Thus a square containing the number 4 has a value of 16. Find a block two squares wide and two squares high with a total value of exactly 50.

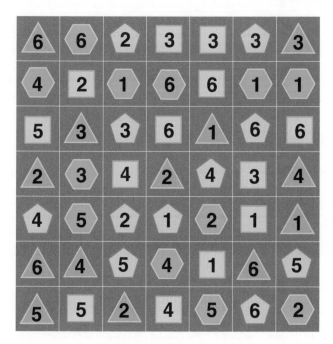

Answer on page 333

Boxes

Playing the game of boxes, each player takes it in turns to join two adjacent dots with a line. If a player's line completes a box, the player wins the box and has another go. It's your turn in the game below. To avoid giving your opponent a lot of boxes, what's your best move?

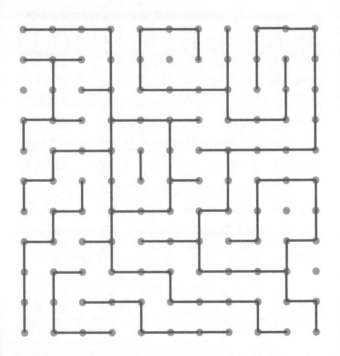

Answer on page 333

Tree Tent

Every tree 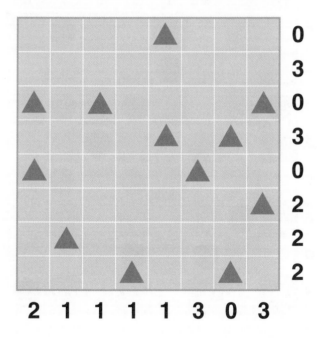 has one tent found horizontally or vertically adjacent to it. No tent can be in an adjacent square to another tent (even diagonally). The numbers by each row and column tell you how many tents are there. Can you locate all the tents?

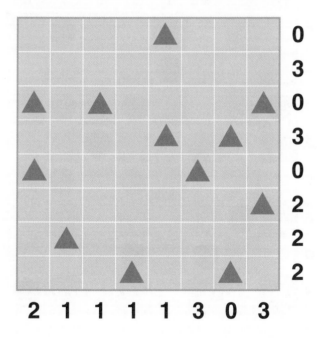

Checkers

Make a move for white so that eight black pieces are left, none of which are in the same column or row.

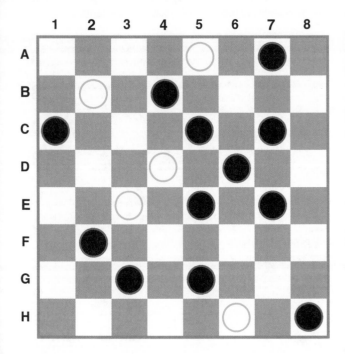

Answer on page 333

Dice Puzzle

What's the missing number?

15 12 16 ?

Answer on page 333

Figure it Out

The sequence 23224 can be found once in the grid, reading up, down, backwards, forwards or diagonally. Can you pick it out?

4	2	2	3	4	4	4	4	3	4	4	4
4	4	3	4	2	2	2	2	2	2	2	2
2	3	2	2	3	3	3	2	4	3	3	3
3	2	3	2	2	3	2	2	2	2	2	2
3	4	3	2	2	2	4	3	2	2	4	2
3	3	2	2	3	3	4	2	2	3	2	2
4	3	2	2	2	2	2	3	2	2	3	3
2	4	3	3	4	3	2	2	3	4	3	4
3	4	4	4	2	2	2	3	2	2	2	2
4	2	2	2	2	3	3	2	4	3	3	3
2	4	3	2	4	4	4	4	2	2	2	2
3	2	3	2	2	3	4	3	3	2	3	4

Answer on page 334

Game of Three Halves

Which three shapes below will piece together to create the top shape?

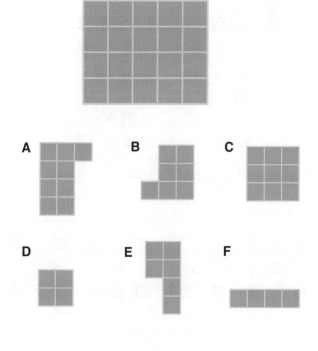

A

B

C

D

E

F

Answer on page 334

Gridlock

Which square correctly completes the grid?

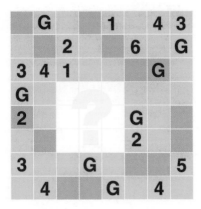

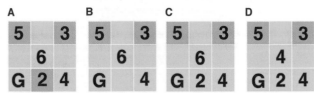

A   B   C   D

Answer on page 334

Latin Square

Complete the grid so that every row and column, and every outlined area, contains the letters A, B, C, D, E and F.

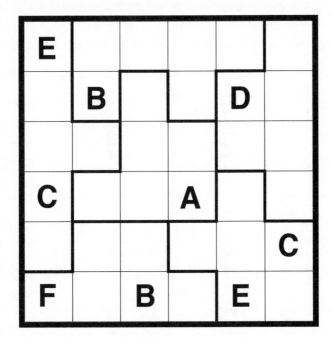

Answer on page 334

Looplink

Connect adjacent dots with either horizontal or vertical lines to create a continuous unbroken loop which never crosses over itself. Some, but not all of the boxes are numbered. The numbers in these boxes tell you how many sides of that box are used by your unbroken line.

Answer on page 334

Masyu

Draw a single unbroken line around the grid that passes through all the circles. The line must enter and leave each box in the centre of one of its four sides. Black Circle: Turn left or right in the box, and the line must pass straight through the next and previous boxes. White Circle: Travel straight through the box, and the line must turn in the next and/or previous box.

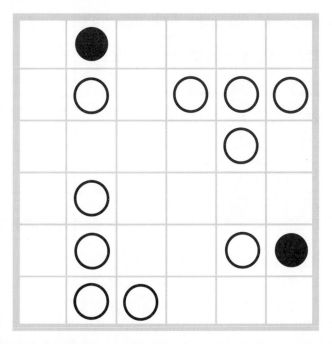

Answer on page 334

Matrix

Which of the boxed figures completes the set?

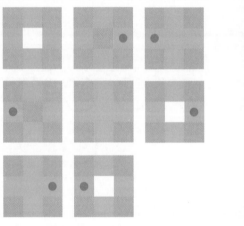 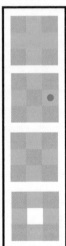

Answer on page 334

Mirror Image

Only one of these pictures is an exact mirror image of the first one. Can you spot it?

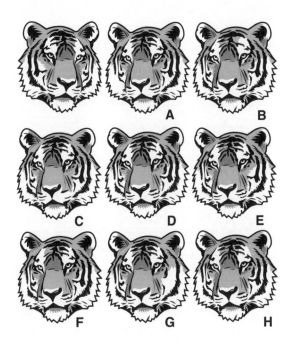

A

B

C

D

E

F

G

H

Answer on page 335

More or Less

The arrows indicate whether a number in a box is greater or smaller than an adjacent number. Complete the grid so that all rows and columns contain the numbers 1 to 6.

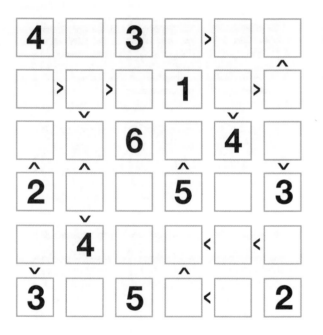

Answer on page 335

Odd One Out

Which of the shapes below is not the same as the other ones?

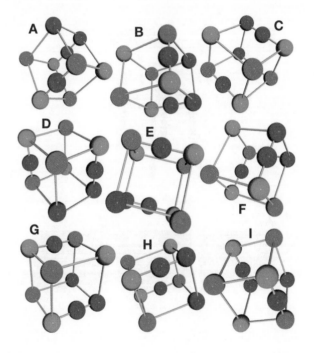

Answer on page 335

Picture Parts

Which box has exactly the right bits to make the pic?

A   **B**   **C**

Answer on page 335

Pots of Dots

How many dots should there be in the hole in this pattern?

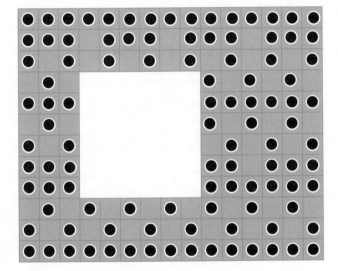

Answer on page 335

Riddle

Little Joe was saving up for a scarf to wear to the big football match. On the first day of he month, he saved one penny, on the second, 2, on the third, 3 and so on until on the day of the match he had exactly the three pounds required to buy the scarf. What day was the game?

Answer on page 335

Safecracker

To open the safe, all the buttons must be pressed in the correct order before the "open" button is pressed. What is the first button pressed in your sequence?

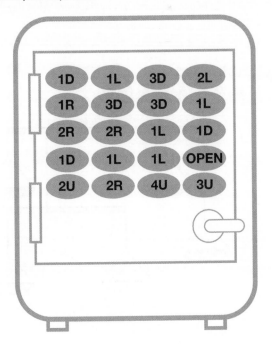

1D	1L	3D	2L
1R	3D	3D	1L
2R	2R	1L	1D
1D	1L	1L	OPEN
2U	2R	4U	3U

Answer on page 335

Scales

Can you arranged the supplied weights in such a way as to balance the whole scale?

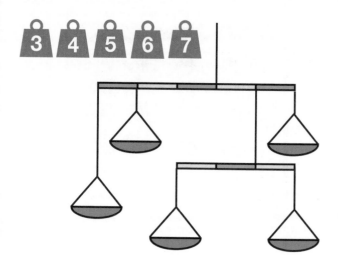

Answer on page 335

Shape Shifting

Fill in the empty squares so that each row, column and long diagonal contains five different coloured balls.

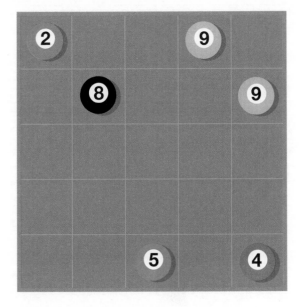

Answer on page 335

Signpost

Can you crack the logical secret behind the distances to these great cities, and work out how far it is to Vancouver?

GENEVA 34

EDINBURGH 17

VANCOUVER ?

TALLINN 86

SANTIAGO 80

Answer on page 336

Spot the Difference

Can you spot ten differences between this pair of pictures?

Answer on page 336

Sudoku Sixpack

Complete the grid so that every row, column and long diagonal contains the numbers 1, 2, 3, 4, 5 and 6.

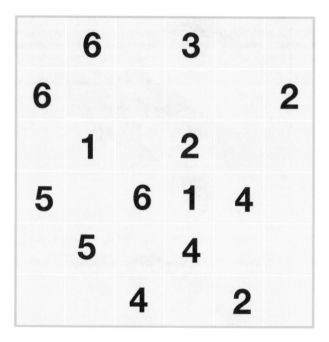

Answer on page 336

Sum People

Work out what number is represented by which person and fill in the question mark.

26 16 ? 21

Answer on page 336

Think of a Number

Officers Kaplutski and Wojowitz were counting up how many jaywalkers they had arrested in a week. Kaplutski was happy to discover he was ahead 14 to 11. Can you express the two cops success rate as a percentage?

Answer on page 336

Venn Diagrams

Can you work out which areas of this diagram represent Australian teetotal surfers who don't play rugby, and non-Australian beer drinking rugby players that don't surf?

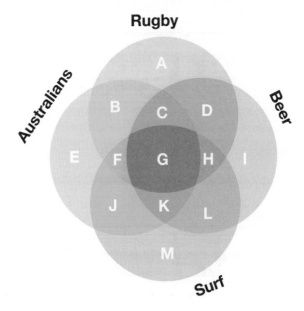

Answer on page 336

Weigh to Go

The coloured balls represent the numbers 1, 2, 3, 4 and 5. Can you work out which is which, and therefore how many purple balls are required to balance the final scale?

Answer on page 336

Matrix

Which of the boxed figures completes the set?

Answer on page 336

Where's the Pair?

Only two of the shapes below are exactly the same – can you find the matching pair?

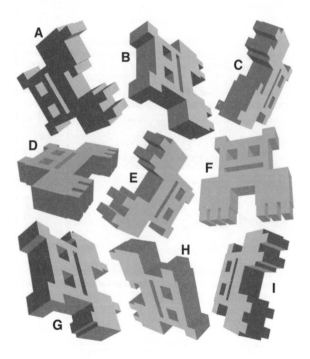

Answer on page 337

All Change

The colour of each triangle in pattern B is directly related to the colours in pattern A. Can you apply the same rules and fill in pattern C?

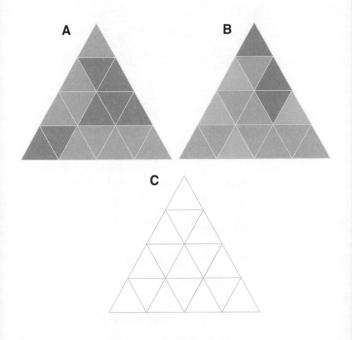

A

B

C

Answer on page 337

Bits and Pieces

These ten pieces can be asembled to spell the name of a movie star... Who?

Answer on page 337

Cube Route

Can you crack the colour code and make your way from one orange square to the other? The blue arrow tells you which way is up...

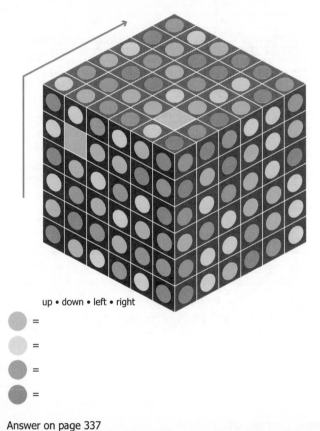

up • down • left • right

⬤ =

⬤ =

⬤ =

⬤ =

Answer on page 337

Finding Nemo

The word NEMO can be found once in the grid, reading up, down, backwards, forwards or diagonally. Can you pick it out?

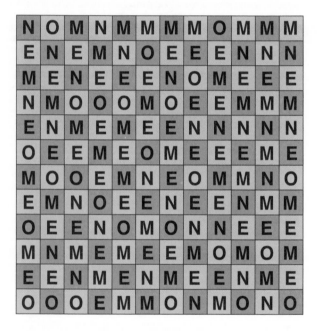

Answer on page 337

Hue Goes There

Three of the sections below can be found in our main grid, one cannot. Can you spot the section that doesn't belong? Beware, the sections might not be the same way round!

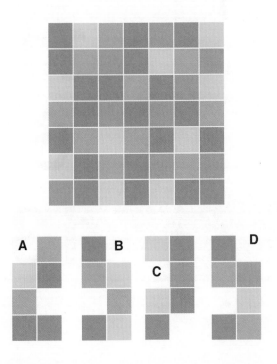

A

B

C

D

Answer on page 337

Magic Squares

Complete the square using nine consecutive numbers, so that all rows, columns and large diagonals add up to the same total.

Answer on page 337

Matrix

Which of the boxed figures completes the set?

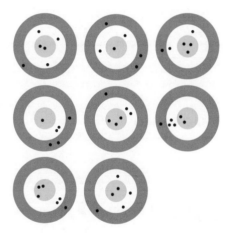 

Answer on page 337

Odd Clocks

Auckland is 16 hours ahead of Sao Paulo, which is 1 hour ahead of Miami. It is 2.15 pm on Saturday in Sao Paulo – what time is it in the other two cities?

SAO PAULO

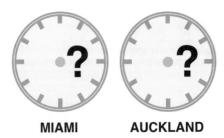

MIAMI **AUCKLAND**

Answer on page 338

Riddle

Jessica promised Julia that she would tell her a huge piece of gossip, but it would have to wait until the day before four days from the day after tomorrow. Today is Wednesday the 3rd – when does Julia get to know?

Answer on page 338

Safecracker

To open the safe, all the buttons must be pressed in the correct order before the "open" button is pressed. What is the first button pressed in your sequence?

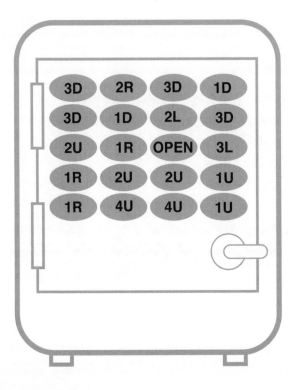

3D	2R	3D	1D
3D	1D	2L	3D
2U	1R	OPEN	3L
1R	2U	2U	1U
1R	4U	4U	1U

Answer on page 338

Logic Sequence

The balls below have been rearranged. Can you work out the new sequence of the balls from the clues given below?

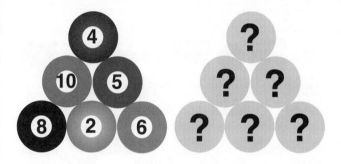

The 4 ball isn't touching the 5 or the 2.
The 8 ball is touching four others.
The 4 ball is immediately to the right of the 6.
The 10 ball is resting on two balls totalling 13.

Answer on page 338

Knight's Move

Find an empty square in the grid that is one chess knight's move away from a blue, red and yellow circle. A knight's move is an 'L' shape – two squares sideways, up or down in any direction, followed by one square to the left or right.

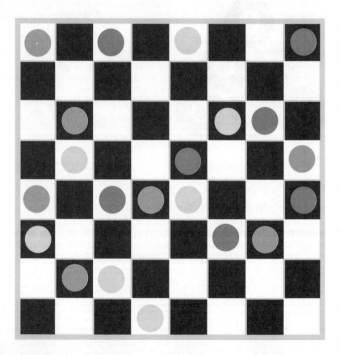

Answer on page 338

Boxes

Playing the game of boxes, each player takes it in turns to join two adjacent dots with a line. If a player's line completes a box, the player wins the box and has another go. It's your turn in the game below. To avoid giving your opponent a lot of boxes, what's your best move?

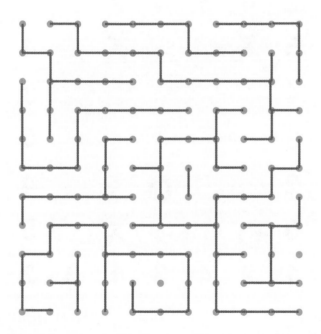

Answer on page 338

X and O

The numbers around the edge of the grid describe the number of X's in the vertical, horizontal and diagonal lines connecting with that square. Complete the grid so that there is an X or O in every square.

2	4	5	4	2	7	1
5	X			X		4
4						3
3						6
2			O			4
5	O			X		5
1	2	4	3	4	6	2

Answer on page 338

Think Back

Study these images for a minute, then cover them and answer the five questions below.

Questions:
1. How many of the yellow stars are on blue circles?
2. How many red circles are there?
3. Counting stars, circles and backgrounds, how many are blue in total?
4. What colour background has the red circle?
5. What colour star has the yellow background?

Answer on page 338

Sudoku

Fill in each row, column and 9x9 box with the numbers 1, 2, 3, 4, 5, 6, 7, 8, 9 once only.

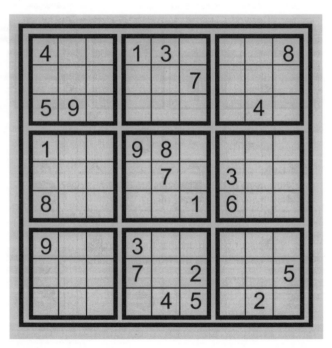

Answer on page 339

Spot the Difference

Can you spot ten differences between this pair of pictures?

Answer on page 339

Same Difference

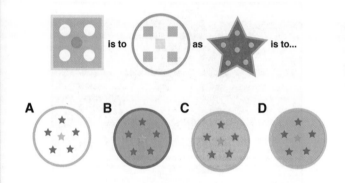

A **B** **C** **D**

Answer on page 339

Percentage Point

What percentage of this shape is blue and what percentage is orange?

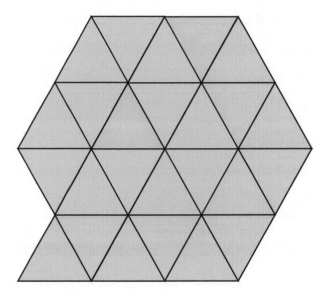

Answer on page 339

Pots of Dots

How many dots should there be in the hole in this pattern?

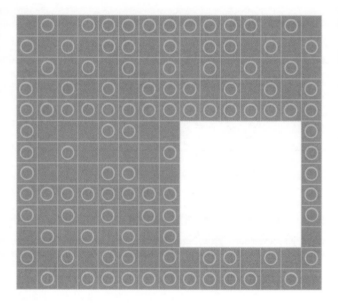

Answer on page 339

Checkers

Make a move for white so that eight black pieces are left, none of which are in the same column or row.

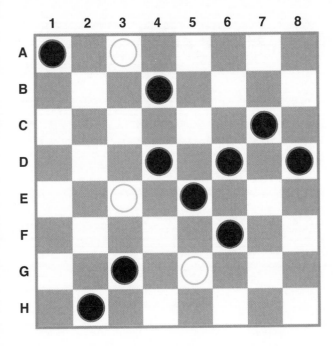

Answer on page 339

Follow That

The sequence below follows a logical pattern. Can you work out what colour face follows, and if it should be smiling?

 **?**

Answer on page 339

Latin Square

Complete the grid so that every row and column, and every outlined area, contains the letters A, B, C, D, E and F.

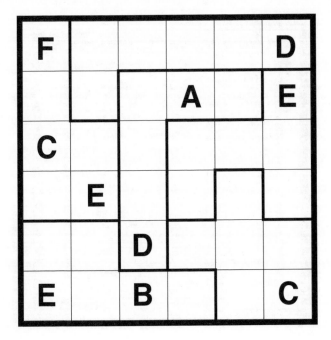

Answer on page 339

Location

Below is an altered view of a world-famous landmark. Can you tell where it is?

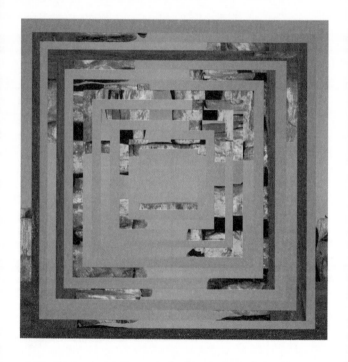

Answer on page 340

Matrix

Which of the boxed figures completes the set?

Answer on page 340

Piece Puzzle

Only one of these pieces fits the hole in our main
picture – the others have all been altered slightly by our artist.
Can you place the missing pic?

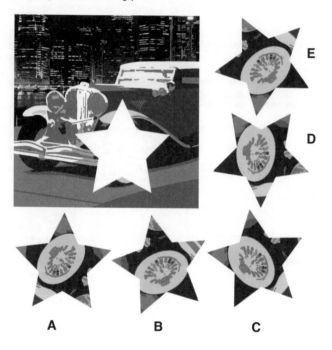

A   B   C

Answer on page 340

268

Pool Puzzle

You're playing stripes in a game of pool, and you've cleaned up all your balls. You're snookered on the black though... Can you spot the shot?

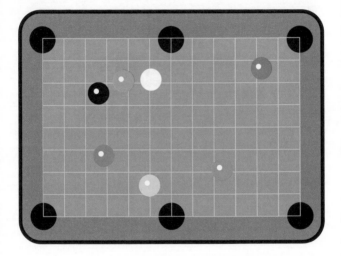

Answer on page 340

Number Mountain

Replace the question marks with numbers so that each pair of blocks adds up to the block directly above them.

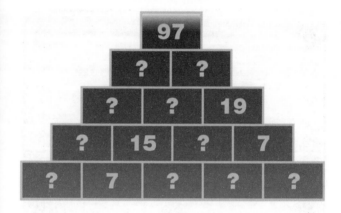

Answer on page 340

Picture Parts

Which box has exactly the right bits to make the pic?

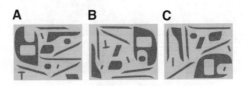

A   B   C

Answer on page 340

Riddle

Belinda, Benny, Bobby, Brian and Bill entered a competition to guess how many sweets there were in a jar. Belinda said 300, Ben said 280, Bobby said 290, Brian said 250 and Bill said 260. Two guesses were just ten sweets away from the number. One guess was 40 away and another was wrong by 30. But who won?

Answer on page 340

Sudoku

Complete the grid so that all rows and columns, and each outlined block of nine squares, contain the numbers 1, 2, 3, 4, 5, 6, 7, 8 and 9.

	6	2			8	5		7
1				3		9		
	8			9			2	
	7			8		3	4	
			1		5			
5						8	1	6
2	1		6	5		7		
		3						
8				2	3		9	1

Answer on page 340

Sum People

Work out what number is represented by which person and fill in the question mark.

Answer on page 341

Think of a Number

Old Mother Jones loves her gummy sweets. They come in three colours: orange, red and yellow. There were exactly twice as many red sweets as yellow ones in the packet. After eating seven orange ones, she had one less orange than yellow left, and the number of orange sweets remaining represented 20 percent of the sweets she started with. How many did she start with?

Answer on page 341

Weigh to Go

The coloured balls represent the numbers 1, 2, 3, 4 and 5. Can you work out which is which, and therefore how many red balls are required to balance the final scale?

Answer on page 341

Rainbow Reckoning

The crazy paving around this fountain will use just Gold, Black and Cream stones. No two stones that touch each other can be the same colour. What colour will the stone under the proposed sundial?

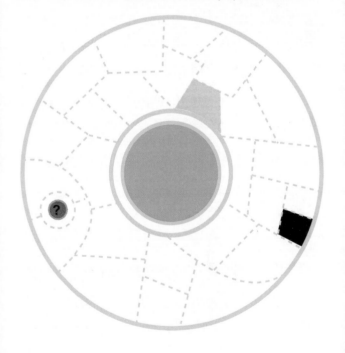

Answer on page 341

Shuffle

Fill up the shuffle box so that each row, column and long diagonal contains a Jack, Queen, King and Ace of each suit.

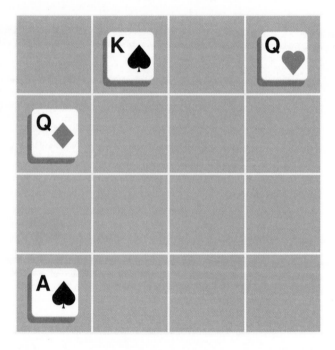

Answer on page 341

Mini Nonogram

The numbers by each row and column describe black squares and groups of black squares that are adjoining. Colour in all the black squares and a six number combination will be revealed.

							1				
							1				
		1					1	1			
	1	1	3				1	3			
	3	1	1		5		1	1		1	
	1	1	5		5		1	3	1	5	5

| 3 3 3 |
| 1 1 1 |
| 3 3 1 |
| 1 1 1 1 |
| 3 3 1 |
| |
| 3 3 1 |
| 1 1 1 |
| 1 3 1 |
| 1 1 1 1 |
| 1 3 1 |

Answer on page 341

Double Drat

All these shapes appear twice in the box except one. Can you spot the singleton?

Answer on page 341

Where's the Pair?

Only two of these pictures are exactly the same. Can you spot the matching pair?

Answer on page 341

The Red Corner

Use the red corners to make the central number the same way in all three cases. What number should replace the question mark?

  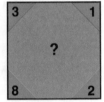

Answer on page 342

Hub Signs

What numbers should appear in the hubs of these number wheels?

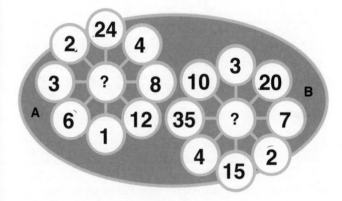

Answer on page 342

Box It

The value of each shape is the number of sides each shape has, multiplied by the number within it. Thus a square containing the number 4 has a value of 16. Find a block two squares wide and two squares high with a total value of exactly 100.

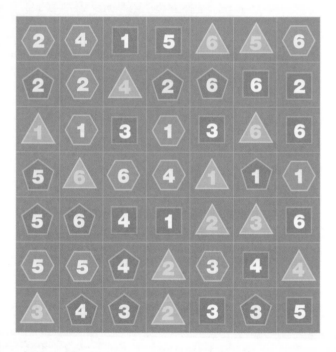

Answer on page 342

Revolutions

Cog A has 10 teeth, cog B has 8 and cog C has 14. How many revolutions must cog A turn through to bring all three cogs back to these exact positions?

Answer on page 342

Riddle

Ada the antique dealer was pondering her profits one day, and thinking how she could improve them. She looked at the Victorian clock she was selling for a 5% profit, and worked out that had she bought it for 10% less and sold it at the same price she would have made a £15 profit. How much did she buy it for?

Answer on page 342

All Change

The colour of each square in pattern B is directly related to the colours in pattern A. The square colours in pattern C relate to pattern B the same way. Can you apply the same the rules and fill in pattern D?

A

B

C

D

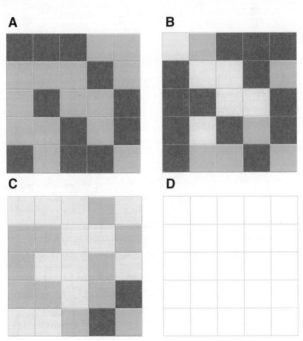

Answer on page 342

Where's the Pair?

Only two of the shapes below are exactly the same, can you find the matching pair?

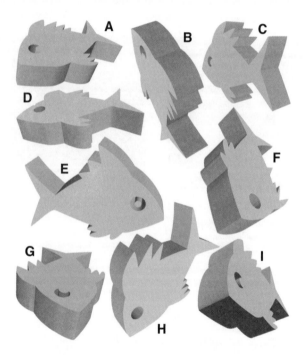

Answer on page 342

All Change

The colour of each hexagon in pattern B is directly related to the colours in pattern A. Can you apply the same rules and fill in pattern C?

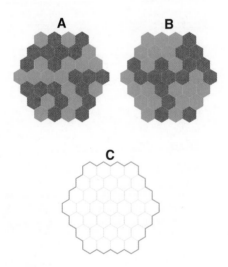

Answer on page 342

Cats and Cogs

Turn the handle in the indicated direction... Does the cat go up or down?

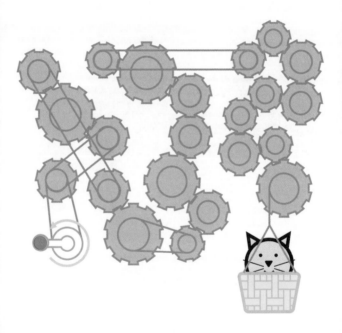

Answer on page 343

Cut and Fold

Which of the patterns below is created by this fold and cut?

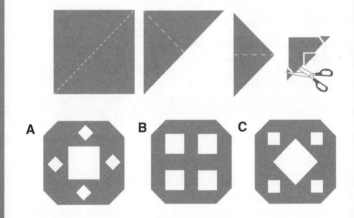

A

B

C

Answer on page 343

Get the Picture

These two grids, when merged together, will make a picture... Of what?

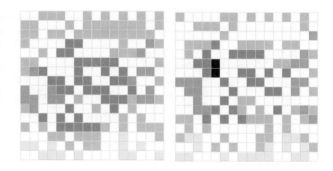

Answer on page 343

More or Less

The arrows indicate whether a number in a box is greater or smaller than an adjacent number. Complete the grid so that all rows and columns contain the numbers 1 to 6.

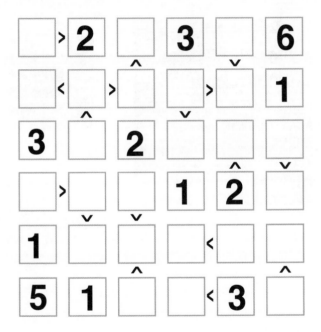

Answer on page 343

Patch of the Day

Place the shape over the grid so that no colour appears twice in the same row or column. Beware, the shape may not be the right way up!

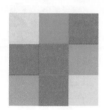

Answer on page 343

Riddle

Mr and Mrs Toggle were driving from Aystown to Beestown on vacation when Mr T accidentally ran down a signpost at a road junction. The post was fine, completely unharmed. But how do they know which way Beestown is now?

Answer on page 343

Scene It?

The four squares below can all be found in the picture grid – can you track them down? Beware, they may not be the right way up!

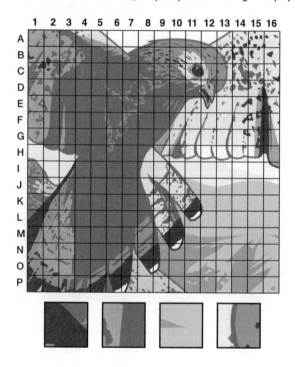

Answer on page 343

Shape Shifting

Fill in the empty squares so that each row, column and long diagonal contains six different symbols

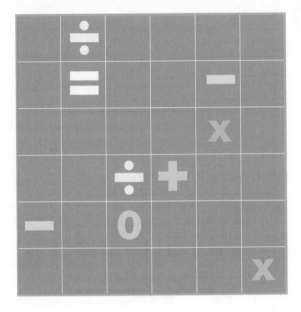

Answer on page 343

Sudoku

Complet the grid so that all rows and columns, and each outlined block of nine squares, contain the numbers 1, 2, 3, 4, 5, 6, 7, 8 and 9.

5	1			2		4	9	8
	3		1		6		7	5
	8				4	6		
	7	3			9		8	
1				7		9		2
	2		3		5	1		
	5		8	6			4	
	9	2					5	6
8		4		9	7	3		

Answer on page 344

Block Party

Assuming all blocks that are not visible from this angle are present, how many blocks have been removed from this 5 x 5 x 5 cube?

Answer on page 344

Chess

Can you place a queen, a bishop, a knight and a rook on this chessboard board so that the red squares are attacked by exactly two pieces, and the green ones by 3 pieces?

Answer on page 344

Double Maze

Make your way from A to B without passing through any yellow squares – then do it again without passing through any blue squares!

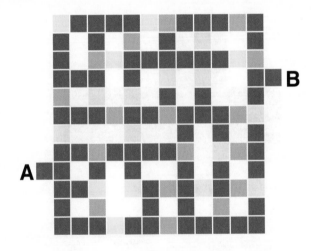

Answer on page 344

Cubism

The shape below can be folded to make a cube. Which of the four cubes picured below could it make?

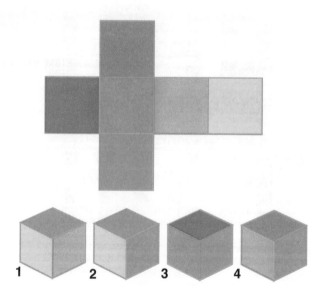

1   2   3   4

Answer on page 344

Odd One Out

Which of the shapes below is not the same as the other ones?

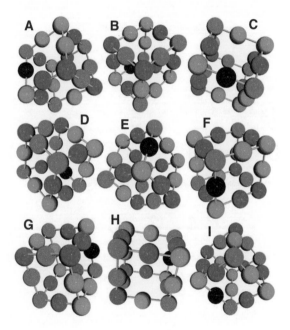

Answer on page 344

Radar

The numbers in some cells in the grid indicate the exact number of black cells that should border it. Shade these black, until all the numbers are surrounded by the correct number of black cells.

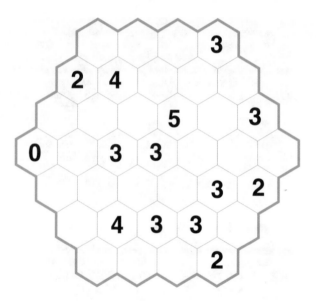

Answer on page 344

Shuffle

Fill up the shuffle box so that each row, column and long diagonal contains a Jack, Queen, King and Ace of each suit.

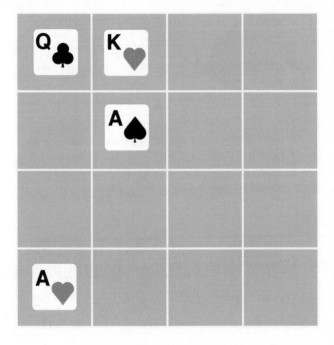

Answer on page 344

Silhouette

Which of the coloured in pics matches our silhouette?

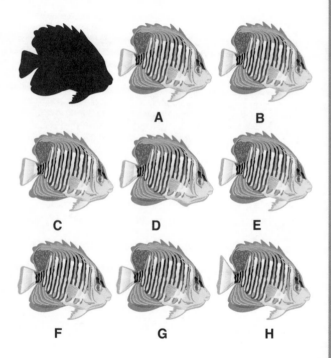

A

B

C

D

E

F

G

H

Answer on page 345

306

Symbol Sums

These symbols represent the numbers 1 to 4. If the pink parrot represents the number 2, can you work out what the other colour parrots are representing and make a working sum?

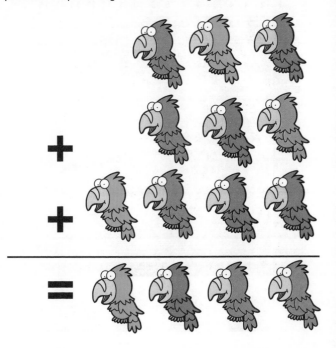

Scene It?

The four squares below can all be found in the picture grid – can you track them down? Beware, they may not be the right way up!

Answer on page 345

In the Area

Can you work out the approximate area that this camel is occupying?

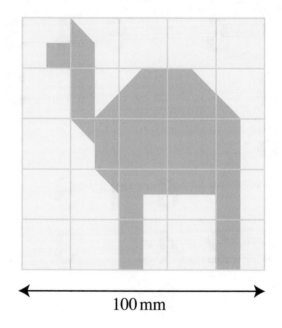

100 mm

Answer on page 345

Sudoku Sixpack

Complete the grid so that every row, column and long diagonal contains the numbers 1, 2, 3, 4, 5 and 6.

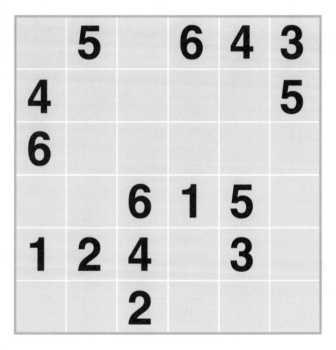

Answer on page 345

Tents and Trees

Every tree ▲ has one tent ▲ found horizontally or vertically adjacent to it. No tent can be in an adjacent square to another tent (even diagonally!). The numbers by each row and column tell you how many tents are there. Can you locate all the tents?

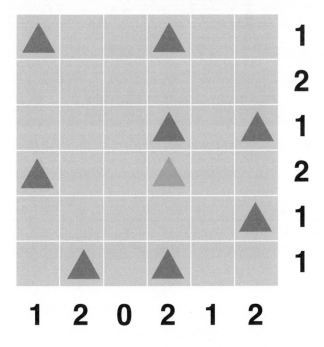

Answer on page 345

Swatch Switch

One of our swatches is missing! Can you work out the four colour sequence that completes the set?

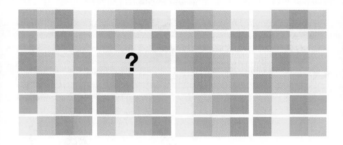

Answer on page 345

Floor Fillers

Below is a plan of the entrance pathway to a theatre, complete with spaces either side for plant pots. Below are some oddly shaped pieces of red carpet... Can you fill the floor with them?

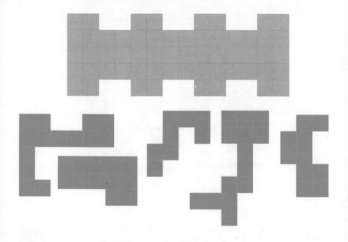

Answer on page 345

Gridlock

Which square correctly completes the grid?

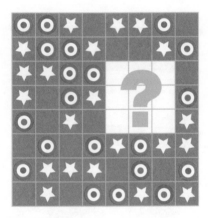

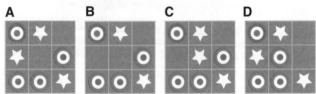

A   **B**   **C**   **D**

Answer on page 346

Looplink

Connect adjacent dots with either horizontal or vertical lines to create a continuous unbroken loop which never crosses over itself. The numbers in these boxes tell you how many sides of that box are used by your unbroken line.

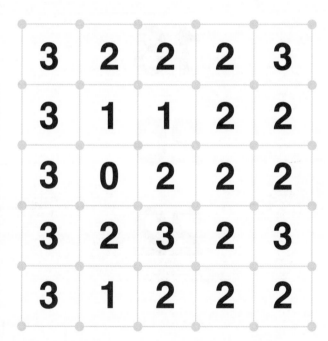

3	2	2	2	3
3	1	1	2	2
3	0	2	2	2
3	2	3	2	3
3	1	2	2	2

Answer on page 346

Magic Squares

Complete the square using nine consecutive numbers, so that all rows, columns and large diagonals add up to the same total.

Answer on page 346

Shape Stacker

Can you work out the logic behind the numbers in these shapes, and suggest what number the question mark represents?

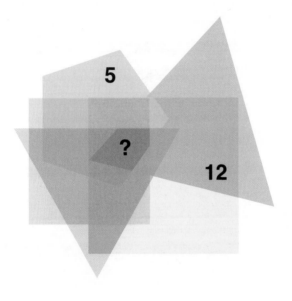

Answer on page 346

Odd Clocks

Rio is 6 hours behind Athens, which is 2 hours behind Karachi.
It is 1.25 am on Thursday in Athens – what time is it in the other
two cities?

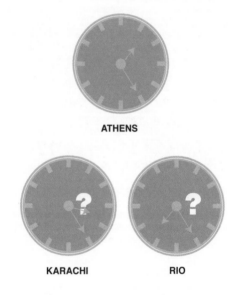

ATHENS

KARACHI

RIO

Answer on page 346

Picture Parts

Which box has exactly the right bits to make the pic?

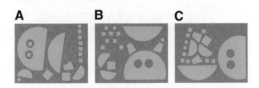

Answer on page 346

Signpost

Can you crack the logical secret behind the distances to these great cities, and work out how far it is to Hong Kong?

NEW YORK 28

GLASGOW 14

HONG KONG ?

BARCELONA 8

COLOMBO 9

Answer on page 346

Matrix

Which of the boxed figures completes the set?

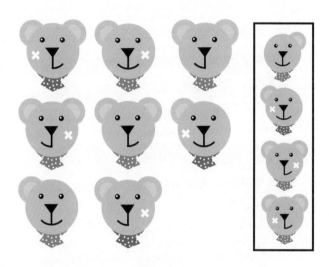

Answer on page 346

Mirror Image

Only one of these pictures is an exact mirror image of the first one?
Can you spot it?

Answer on page 347

Number Sweep

The numbers in some squares in the grid indicate the exact number of black squares that should surround it. Shade these squares until all the numbers are surrounded by the correct number of black squares, and a number will be revealed!

0	2		5		5		5		5		2
	4			8		8		8		5	
2		7	8		6		5		5		2
	5		8			6		6		3	
4		8		7	6		5		4		1
	7		7		5			7		5	
3		5		4		3	5		8		4
	6		4		0		3			8	
3		5		4		3		6	8		5
	7		7		5		6		8		
3		6		8		8		7		4	3
	2		4		5		5		4		1

Answer on page 347

Scales

The arms of these scales are divided into sections – a weight two sections away from the middle will be twice as heavy as a weight one section away. Can you arranged the supplied weights in such a way as to balance the whole scale?

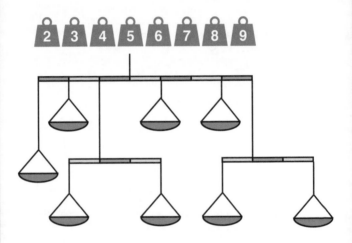

Answer on page 347

Spot the Difference

Can you spot ten differences between this pair of pictures?

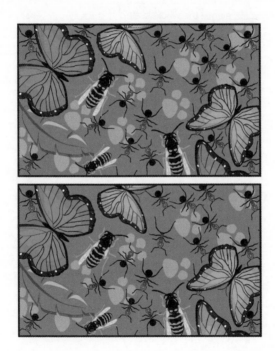

Answer on page 347

Sudoku

Complete the grid so that all rows and columns, and each outlined block of nine squares, contain the numbers 1, 2, 3, 4, 5, 6, 7, 8 and 9.

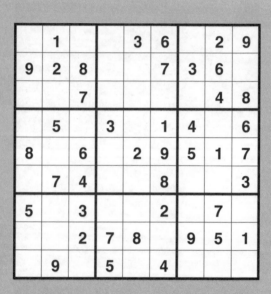

Answer on page 347

Spot the Difference

Can you spot ten differences between this pair of pictures?

Answer on page 347

Answers

Page 178
Answer: E

Page 179

Solution: A line on the top or bottom of this square will only give up one box to your opponent

Page 180
Answer: A

Page 181
Answer:
Blue = Left
Red = Right
Green = Up
Yellow = Down
The final die in your trip is the

Blue 1, three dice down in the second column

Page 182
Answer: A red 2. Two numbers the same are followed by a red number. Two numbers of different colours are followed by a 2

Page 183

Page 184

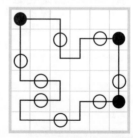

Answers

Page 185

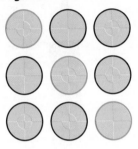

Solution: Each vertical and horizontal line contains one shape with a red outline and two shapes with a black outline. Each line also contains one shape where the inner quartered circle has been removed and one shape that has been rotated through 90 degrees. The missing shape should not be rotated, it should have a red outline and the inner circle should be missing

Page 186

Solution: Each line contains two pyramids with golden balls on top, and one without.

Each line contains two pyramids with a blue 'B', and one without.

Each line contains two pyramids with a hole and one without.

Each line contains one image that has been rotated through 90 degrees.

The missing image should be a pyramid with a golden ball on top, without a blue 'B', but with a hole, and rotated through 90 degrees

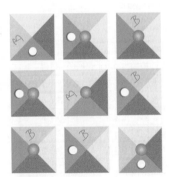

Page 187

Answer: F is the odd one out

Answers

Page 188
Answer: 10. On the 10th jump he makes it!

Page 189
Answer: I15, 19, A9, M1

Page 190
Answer: Two thirds and one third. 351 divided by 3 is 117 (39 + 78) 117 × 2 = 234 (203 + 31)

Page 191
Answer: Purple = 1, Green = 2, Red = 3, Yellow = 4, Blue = 5. Four Yellow balls are required

Page 192

9	8	2	3	1	7	4	5	6
6	5	1	2	9	4	7	3	8
7	4	3	5	6	8	2	1	9
8	6	7	9	2	1	3	4	5
3	2	5	4	8	6	9	7	1
1	9	4	7	3	5	6	8	2
5	1	9	6	4	3	8	2	7
4	7	6	8	5	2	1	9	3
2	3	8	1	7	9	5	6	4

Page 193
Solution: 16

 2

 3

 4

 5

Page 194

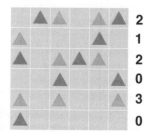

2
1
2
0
3
0

2 0 3 0 2 1

Answers

Page 195
Answer: 42
Score one for a consonant and two for a vowel, then multiply the totals together.
$6 \times 7 = 42$

Page 196
Answer: E

Page 197
Answer: 68

Page 198
Answer: B and H are the pair

Page 199

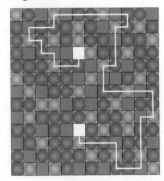

Page 200

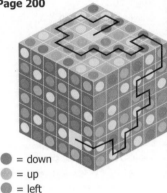

⬤ = down
⬤ = up
⬤ = left
⬤ = right

Page 201

Page 202

Answers

Page 203
Answer: C is the odd shape out

Page 204
Solution: Each vertical and horizontal line contains one shape with a small yellow inner square, one with a small white inner square, and one with a small orange inner square. Each vertical and horizontal line also contains one shape with a larger yellow square, one with a larger white square, and one with a larger orange square. The missing shape must contain a small yellow inner square and a larger yellow square. Of course orange squares are invisible against an orange background

Page 205

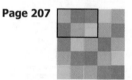

Page 206

2 ‹ 3	1	5 › 4
5	1	4	3	2
4 ‹ 5	2	1	3
3 › 2	5	4	1
1 ‹ 4	3 › 2	5

Page 207

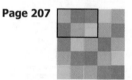

Page 208
44% is blue, 56% is yellow. 11 out of 25 squares in the grid are blue, 14 are yellow. Multiply both numbers by 4 and you see a percentage

Page 209
Answer: Thursday. The goat is lying!

332

Answers

Page 210
Answer: D6, O10, N3, I1

Page 211

Page 212
Answer: B

Page 213

Page 214

Solution: A line on the left or bottom of this square will only give up one box to your opponent

Page 215

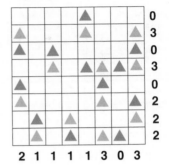

Page 216

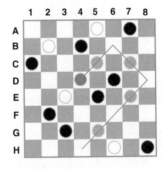

Page 217
Answer: 4. Subtract the right face from the front face and multiply by the top one

333

Answers

Page 218

4	2	2	3	4	4	4	3	4	4	4
4	4	3	4	2	2	2	2	2	2	2
2	3	2	2	3	3	2	4	3	3	3
3	2	3	2	2	3	2	2	2	2	2
3	4	3	2	2	2	4	3	2	2	4	2
3	3	2	2	3	3	4	2	2	3	2	2
4	3	2	2	2	2	2	3	2	2	3	3
2	4	3	3	4	3	2	2	3	4	3	4
3	4	4	4	2	2	2	3	2	2	2	2
4	2	2	2	2	3	3	2	4	3	3	3
2	4	3	2	4	4	4	4	2	2	2	2
3	2	3	2	2	3	4	3	3	2	3	4

Page 219

Solution:
A, B, and D

Page 220

Answer: C. Each row and column in the grid contains two green squares and a letter G, and numbers that total 8

Page 221

E	C	A	D	F	B
A	B	C	E	D	F
D	F	E	B	C	A
C	D	F	A	B	E
B	E	D	F	A	C
F	A	B	C	E	D

Page 222

Page 223

Page 224

Solution: Each vertical and

horizontal line contains one shape with a central green square, one with a central white square, and one with a central pink square.

Each vertical and horizontal line also contains one shape with a blue dot on the left, one with a blue dot on the right, and one with no blue dot. The missing shape should have a central green square and no blue dot

334

Answers

Page 225
Answer: E

Page 226

4	5	3	6 > 2	1

4	5	3	6	2	1
6	3	2	1	5	4
1	2	6	3	4	5
2	6	4	5	1	3
5	4	1	2	3	6
3	1	5	4	6	2

Page 227
Answer: B is the odd one out

Page 228
Answer: A

Page 229
Solution: 25

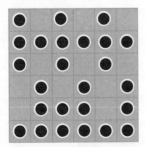

Page 230
Answer: The game was on the 24th day of the month

Page 231

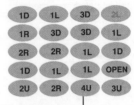

1D	1L	3D	2L
1R	3D	3D	1L
2R	2R	1L	1D
1D	1L	1L	OPEN
2U	2R	4U	3U

Page 232

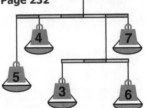

Page 233

2	4	8	9	5
5	8	2	4	9
4	5	9	8	2
9	2	4	5	8
8	9	5	2	4

Answers

Page 234

Answer: 92
Multiply the alphabetical position of the first letter of each city by 5, then subtract the alphabetical position of the last letter 22 x 5 = 110 − 18 = 92

Page 235

Page 236

2	6	5	3	1	4
6	4	1	5	3	2
4	1	3	2	5	6
5	2	6	1	4	3
3	5	2	4	6	1
1	3	4	6	2	5

Page 237

Solution: 20

 1

 3

 7

 12

Page 238

Answer: Kaplutski 56 percent, Wojowitz 44 percent. The total number is 25. Multiply this number, and the others, by 4 to get percentages

Page 239

Answer: J and D

Page 240

Solution: Red = 1, Purple = 2, Green = 3, Blue = 4, Yellow = 5. Five purple balls are required.

Page 241

Answer: Each vertical and horizontal line contains one shape with two stars, one with three, and one with four. Each line also contains one shape a blue moon, one with a pink moon and one with a white moon. Each line also contains one orange sky and two blue ones, and each line contains one moon pointing right and two pointing left. The missing shape should contain

 four stars and a blue sky, and the moon should be white and facing right.

336

Answers

Page 242

Answer: C and H are the pair

Page 243

Solution: If its bordering triangles are predominantly green, a triangle becomes green. If they are predominantly purple, it becomes purple. If the bordering cells are equal in number, the triangle becomes pink, and if the bordering triangles have now become predominantly pink, it also becomes pink

Page 244

Answer: Tom Cruise

Page 245

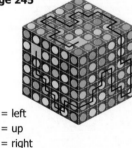

- = left
- = up
- = right
- = down

Page 246

N	O	M	N	M	M	M	M	O	M	M	M
E	N	E	M	N	O	E	E	E	N	N	N
M	E	N	E	E	E	E	N	O	M	E	E
N	M	O	O	O	M	O	E	E	M	M	M
E	N	M	E	M	E	E	N	N	N	N	N
O	E	E	M	E	O	M	E	E	E	M	E
M	O	O	E	M	N	E	O	M	M	N	O
E	M	N	O	E	E	N	E	E	N	M	M
O	E	E	N	O	M	O	N	N	E	E	E
M	N	M	E	M	E	E	M	O	M	O	M
E	E	N	M	E	N	M	E	E	N	M	E
O	O	O	E	M	M	O	N	M	O	N	O

Page 247

Answer: C is the odd shape out

Page 248

7	12	11
14	10	6
9	8	13

Page 249

Solution: Each line contains one target with three holes in the gold, two holes in the white and one hole in the red.

Each line contains one target with three holes in the white, two holes in the gold and one hole in the red. Each line contains one target with three holes in the red, two holes in the white and one hole in the gold. The missing picture must have three holes in the red, two holes in the white and one in the gold

Answers

Page 250
Answer:
1.15 pm on Saturday in Miami
6.15 am on Sunday in Auckland

Page 251
Answer: Monday the 8th

Page 252

3D	2R	3D	1D
3D	1D	2L	3D
2U	1R	OPEN	3L
1R	2U	2U	1U
1R	4U	4U	1U

Page 253

Page 254

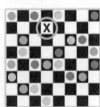

Page 255
Solution: A line on the left or right of this square will only give up one box to your opponent

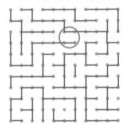

Page 256

2	4	5	4	2	7	1
5	X	X	o	X	o	4
4	o	o	X	o	X	3
3	o	X	o	o	X	6
2	o	X	o	o	X	4
5	o	o	o	X	X	5
1	2	4	3	4	6	2

Page 257
Answers:
1. None
2. 1
3. 3
4. Blue
5. Red

Answers

Page 258

Page **259**

Page 260
Answer: C.
The inner shapes swap with the outer shape. The outer shape's outline colour swaps with that of the central inner shape. The outer shape's colour swaps with that of the other inner shapes

Page 261
Answer: 48% percent is blue, 52% is orange. 12 out of 25 triangles that make up the shape are blue, 13 are orange.

Multiply both numbers by 4 and you see a percentage

Page 262
Solution: 17

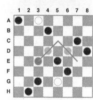

Page 263

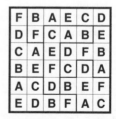

Page 264
Answer: A pink face with a smile. Two different expressions (smile or frown) are followed by a pink face. Two faces the same colour are followed by a smile

Page 265

F	B	A	E	C	D
D	F	C	A	B	E
C	A	E	D	F	B
B	E	F	C	D	A
A	C	D	B	E	F
E	D	B	F	A	C

Answers

Page 266
Answer: Stonehenge

Page 267

Solution: Each vertical and horizontal line contains a picture with one star, a picture with two stars, and a picture with no stars.

Each line contains two full moons and a quarter moon. Each line contains a picture where the far right–hand building has three lights, a picture where it has two lights and a picture where it has one light.

The last picture must have two stars and a quarter moon, and the far right–hand building must have three lights

Page 268
Answer: D

Page 269

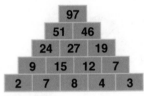

Page 270

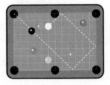

Page 271
Answer: B

Page 272
Answer: Bobby. There are 290 sweets in the jar

Page 273

9	6	2	4	1	8	5	3	7
1	4	5	2	3	7	9	6	8
3	8	7	5	9	6	1	2	4
6	7	1	9	8	2	3	4	5
4	3	8	1	6	5	2	7	9
5	2	9	3	7	4	8	1	6
2	1	4	6	5	9	7	8	3
7	9	3	8	4	1	6	5	2
8	5	6	7	2	3	4	9	1

Answers

Page 274
Solution: 22

 3

 4

 5

 10

Page 275
Answer: 50.
22 red, 11 yellow and
17 orange

Page 276
Answer:
Blue = 1, Yellow = 2, Red = 3,
Purple = 4, Green = 5.
Three red balls are required

Page 277
Answer: Cream

Page 278
Answer:

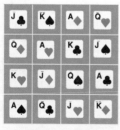

Page 279

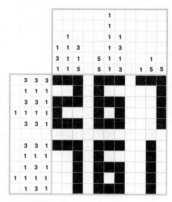

Page 280

Page 281
Answer: A and F are the pair

Answers

Page 282
Answer: Add the top two red corners, then add the bottom two. Then multiply the two totals.
$3 + 1 = 4$.
$8 + 2 = 10$.
$4 \times 10 = 40$.

Page 283
Answers:
A) 24 - multiply the opposite numbers.
B) 5 - divide the opposite numbers.

Page 284

Page 285
Answer: 28 revolutions of cog A, which will make exactly 35 revolutions of cog B and 20 revolutions of cog C.

Page 286
Answer: £100

Page 287
Solution: If its bordering squares (not diagonals) are predominantly pink, a square becomes blue.

If they are predominantly blue it becomes pink. If the bordering squares are equal in number, the square becomes yellow, and if the bordering squares have now become predominantly yellow, it also becomes yellow.

Page 288
Answer: A and I are the pair.

Page 289
Solution: If its bordering cells are predominantly green, a cell becomes grey. If they are predominantly grey, it becomes green. If the bordering cells are equal in number, the colour of a cell changes

Answers

Page 290
Answer: Up

Page 291
Answer: C

Page 292

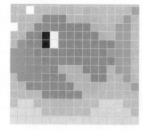

Page 293

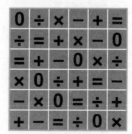

Page 294

Page 295
Answer: Stick the signpost back up. If the sign to Aystown is pointing the way they have just come, then the rest of the signs will be pointing the right way.

Page 296
Answer: L1, E2, M16, C13

Page 297

Answers

Page 298

5	1	6	7	2	3	4	9	8
4	3	9	1	8	6	2	7	5
2	8	7	9	5	4	6	1	3
6	7	3	2	1	9	5	8	4
1	4	5	6	7	8	9	3	2
9	2	8	3	4	5	1	6	7
3	5	1	8	6	2	7	4	9
7	9	2	4	3	1	8	5	6
8	6	4	5	9	7	3	2	1

Page 299
Answer: 49

Page 300

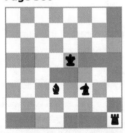

Page 301

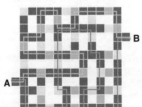

Page 302
Answer: 1

Page 303
Answer: D is the odd one out

Page 304

Page 305

Q♣	K♥	A♦	J♠
J♦	A♠	K♣	Q♥
K♠	Q♦	J♥	A♣
A♥	J♣	Q♠	K♦

344

Answers

Page 306
Answer: F

Page 307
Answer:
purple 1
pink 2
green 3
red 4

Page 308
Answer: P11, B13, M14, H2

Page 309
Answer: 3650 square
millimetres.
Each 20×20 square
represents $400\,mm^2$.
4 squares, 6 half–squares,
2 half–square triangles,
3 quarter–squares and
3 8th of a square triangles
are used

Page 310

2	5	1	6	4	3
4	6	3	2	1	5
6	3	5	4	2	1
3	4	6	1	5	2
1	2	4	5	3	6
5	1	2	3	6	4

Page 311

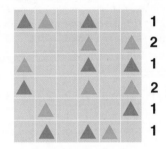

1
2
1
2
1
1

1 2 0 2 1 2

Page 312

Page 313

345

Answers

Page 314

Answer: A. Each row and column in the grid contains three stars, two targets with a red outer ring and one with a blue outer ring

Page 315

3	2	2	2	3
3	1	1	2	2
3	0	2	2	2
3	2	3	2	3
3	1	2	2	2

Page 316

23	18	19
16	20	24
21	22	17

Page 317

Answer: 720
The numbers represent the number of sides in the shape they occupy. When shapes overlap, the numbers are multiplied
3 x 3 x 4 x 4 x 5 = 720

Page 318

Answer:
3.25 am on Thursday in Karachi.
5.25 pm on Wednesday in Rio

Page 319

Answer: A

Page 320

Answer: 16
Multiply the alphabetical position of the first letter of each name by the number of vowels it contains. H = 8 and Hong Kong contains 2 vowels. 8 x 2 = 16

Page 321

Solution: Each horizontal and vertical line contains a red, a blue and a green neckerchief.

Each line contains one one–eared bear. Each line contains a full mouth, a left half–mouth and a right half–mouth. Each line contains two sticking plasters, one left and one right.

The missing picture should have a red neckerchief, have two ears, a right half–mouth and a sticking plaster on the left

346

Answers

Page 322
Answer: H

Page 323

0	2		5		5		5		5		2
		4		8		8		8		5	
2		7	8		6		5		5		2
	5		8			6		6		3	
4		8		7	6		5		4		1
	7		7		5			7		5	
3		5		4		3	5		8		4
	6		4		0		3			8	
3		5		4		3		6	8		5
	7		7		5		6		8		
3		6		8		8		7		4	3
	2		4		5		5		4		1

Page 324

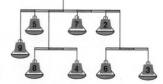

Page 325

Page 326

4	1	5	8	3	6	7	2	9
9	2	8	1	4	7	3	6	5
3	6	7	2	9	5	1	4	8
2	5	9	3	7	1	4	8	6
8	3	6	4	2	9	5	1	7
1	7	4	6	5	8	2	9	3
5	8	3	9	1	2	6	7	4
6	4	2	7	8	3	9	5	1
7	9	1	5	6	4	8	3	2

Page 327

Difficult Puzzles

Odd One Out

Which of the shapes below is not the same as the other ones?

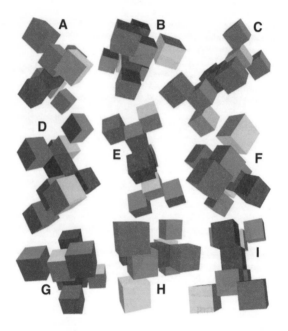

Answer on page 501

Pattern Pairs

Only one of the tiles below is unique; the others all have an exact matching pair. Can you find the one-off?

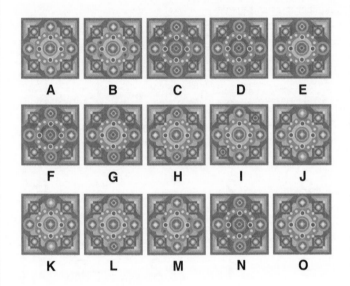

Answer on page 501

Minesweeper

The numbers in some squares in the grid indicate the exact number of black squares that should surround it. Shade these squares until all the numbers are surrounded by the correct number of black squares.

0			1	2			2
1		2	1				2
		2		2	2	2	
2		2					0
	1	1	2		2	1	
2		1		2		2	1
	3			3	5		3
2		2	2				

Answer on page 501

Masyu

Draw a single continuous line around the grid that passes through all the circles. The line must enter and leave each box in the centre of one of its four sides.

Black Circle: Turn left or right in the box, and the line must pass straight through the next and previous boxes.

White Circle: Travel straight through the box, and the line must turn in the next and/or previous box.

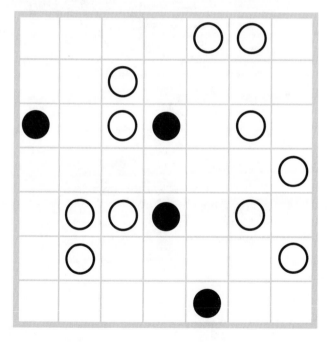

Answer on page 501

Where's the Pair?

Only two of the shapes below are exactly the same, can you find the matching pair?

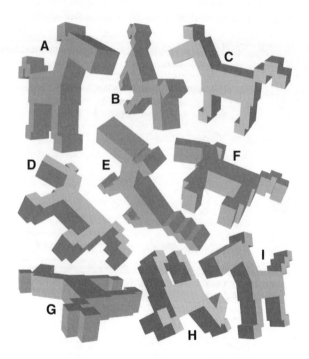

Answer on page 501

All Change

The colour of each hexagon in pattern B is directly related to the colours in pattern A. Can you apply the same rules and fill in pattern C?

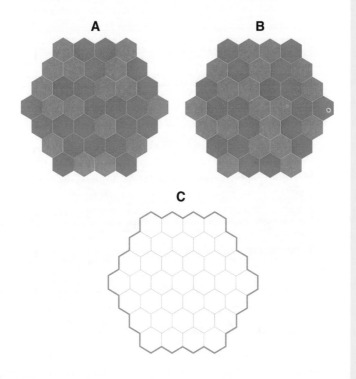

A

B

C

Answer on page 501

Camp Conifer

Every tree 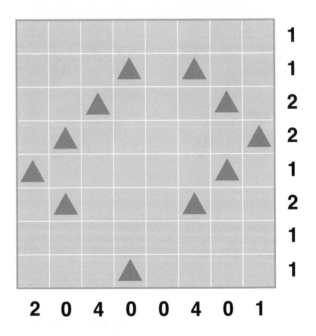 has one tent found horizontally or vertically adjacent to it. No tent can be in an adjacent square to another tent (even diagonally). The numbers by each row and column tell you how many tents are there. Can you locate all the tents?

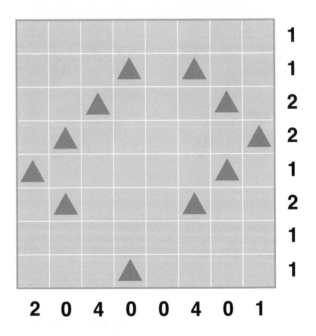

Answer on page 501

Codoku Six

Complete the first grid so that every row and column contains all the letters BCIMU and W. Do the same with grid 2 and the numbers 12345 and 6. To decode the finished grid, add the numbers in the shaded squares to the letters in the matching squares in the first grid (ie: A + 3 = D, Y + 4 = C) to get six new letters which can be arranged to spell the name of a city.

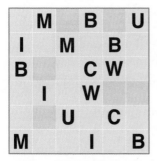
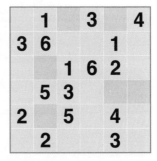

Answer on page 501

Cube Volume

These little cubes originally made a big cube measuring 20 cm × 20 cm × 20 cm. Now some of the little cubes have been removed, can you work out what volume the remaining cubes have now? Assume all invisible cubes are present.

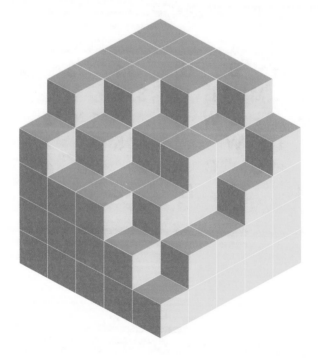

Answer on page 502

The Great Divide

Divide up the grid into four equal sized, equally shaped parts, each containing four circles of four different colours.

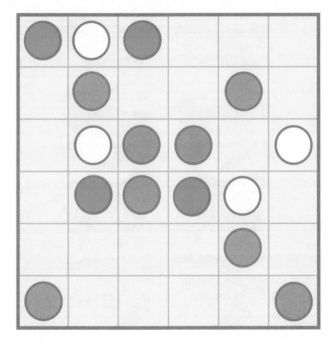

Answer on page 502

Where's the Pair?

Only two of these pictures are exactly the same. Can you spot the matching pair?

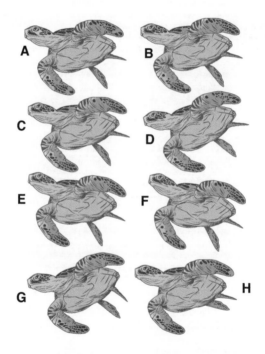

Answer on page 502

Sudoku

Complete the grid so that all rows and columns, and each outlined block of nine squares, contain the numbers 1, 2, 3, 4, 5, 6, 7, 8 and 9.

			3		7			
6	5			9			3	
7			5		8	2	1	
	6			2	1		4	
3			4					
	9				5			
5	1					8		7
						1		
2		8		7		5	6	4

Answer on page 502

Scene It?

The four squares below can all be found in the picture grid – can you track them down? Beware, they may not be the right way up!

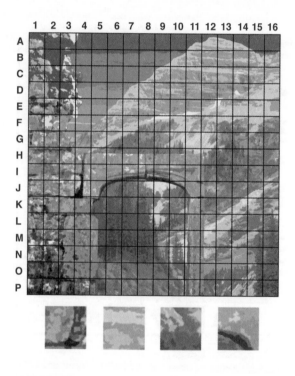

Answer on page 502

Think Back

Study these images for a minute, then cover them up and answer the five questions below.

Questions:
1. How many places in front of the green car is the red car?
2. What number car is second?
3. What is the total of the numbers on the first two cars?
4. What number car is in front of the yellow one?
5. What colour car is directly behind car number 1?

Answer on page 502

Pattern Pairs

Only one of the tiles below is unique; the others all have an exact matching pair. Can you find the one-off?

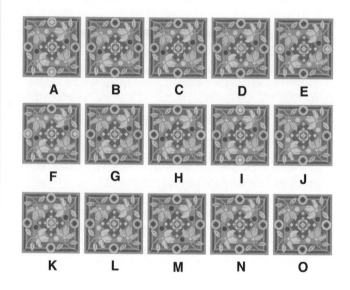

Answer on page 502

Percentage Point

Can you determine what percentage of this honeycomb is occupied by bees, and what percentage of the bees are awake?

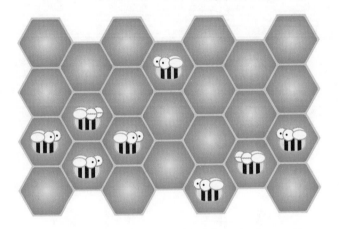

Answer on page 502

Minesweeper

The numbers in some squares in the grid indicate the exact number of black squares that should surround it. Shade these squares until all the numbers are surrounded by the correct number of black squares.

	2	2		2	3		3
2			3				
	3	3		2	3		3
3			3	3		2	2
	3	4			1	2	
1				3			
2	4	4	3		2		
			1	1		2	1

Answer on page 503

Logic Sequence

The balls below have been rearranged. Can you work out the new sequence of the balls from the clues given below?

The square is immediately to the right of the X.
The circle is between the X and the triangle.
There are two balls between the circle and the star.

Answer on page 503

A Piece of Pie

Can you crack the pie code and work out what number belongs where the question mark is?

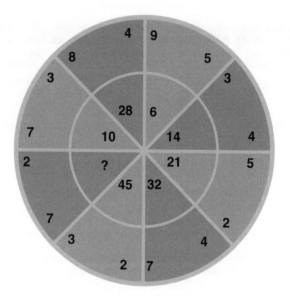

Answer on page 503

All Change

The colour of each triangle in pattern B is directly related to the colours in pattern A. Can you apply the same rules and fill in pattern C?

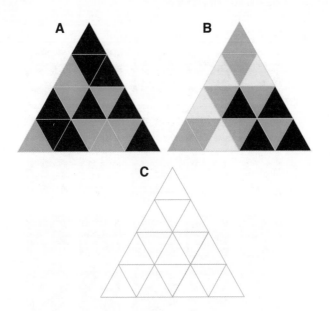

Answer on page 503

Dice Maze

The colours on these dice represent a direction – up, down, left and right. Starting in the middle die of the grid, follow the instructions correctly and you will visit every die in turn once only. What's the last die you visit on your trip?

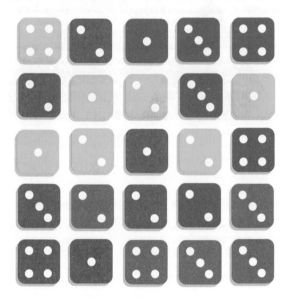

Answer on page 503

Five-Point Problem

Discover the pattern behind the numbers on these pentagons and fill in the blanks to complete the puzzle.

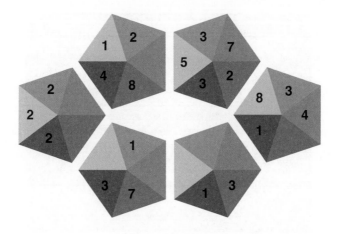

Answer on page 503

The Great Divide

Divide up the grid into four equal sized, equally shaped parts, each containing one each of the four different symbols.

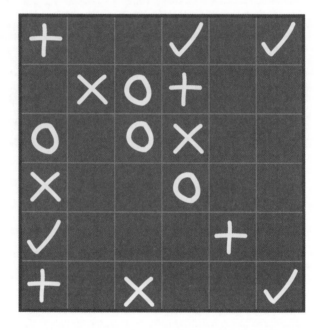

Answer on page 503

Killer Six

Complete the grid so that all rows and columns contain the numbers 1, 2, 3, 4, 5 and 6. Areas with a dotted outline contain numbers that add up to the total shown.

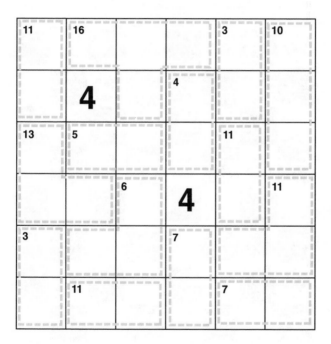

Answer on page 503

Knight's Move

Find an empty square in the grid that is one chess knight's move away from a blue, red and yellow circle. A knight's move is an 'L' shape – two squares sideways, up or down in any direction, followed by one square to the left or right.

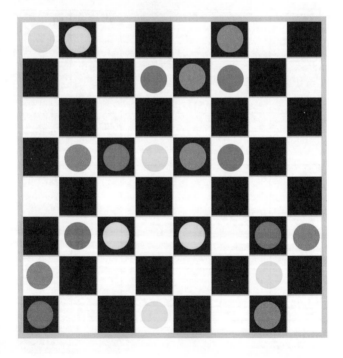

Answer on page 504

Looplink

Connect adjacent dots with either horizontal or vertical lines to create a continuous unbroken loop which never crosses over itself. Some, but not all of the boxes are numbered. The numbers in these boxes tell you how many sides of that box are used by your unbroken line.

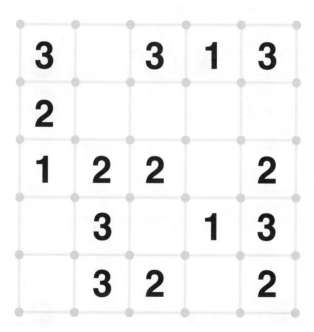

Answer on page 504

Masyu

Draw a single continuous line around the grid that passes through all the circles. The line must enter and leave each box in the centre of one of its four sides.

Black Circle: Turn left or right in the box, and the line must pass straight through the next and previous boxes.

White Circle: Travel straight through the box, and the line must turn in the next and/or previous box.

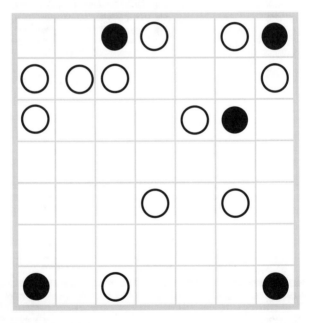

Answer on page 504

Mini Nonogram

The numbers by each row and column describe black squares and groups of black squares that are adjoining. Colour in all the black squares and a six number combination will be revealed.

					1									
					1									
					1									
				5	1	5			5			1		
				5	1	5		3	1	5		1	5	5
		3	1	3										
	1	1	1	1										
		3	1	1										
	1	1	1	1										
		3	1	1										
	3	1	1	1										
1	1	1	1	1										
	1	1	3	1										
	1	1	1	1										
		3	1	1										

Answer on page 504

Mirror Image

Only one of these pictures is an exact mirror image of the first one? Can you spot it?

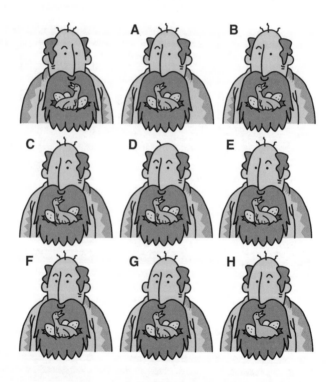

A

B

C

D

E

F

G

H

Answer on page 504

More or Less

The arrows indicate whether a number in a box is greater or smaller than an adjacent number. Complete the grid so that all rows and columns contain the numbers 1 to 5.

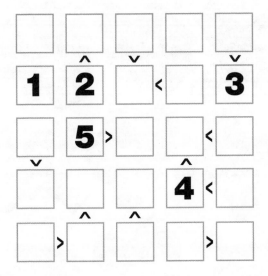

Answer on page 504

Odd One Out

Which of the shapes below is not the same as the other ones?

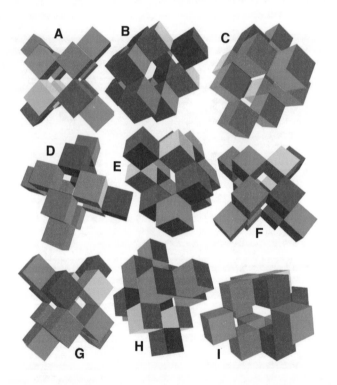

Answer on page 504

Pattern Pairs

Ony one of the tiles below is unique; the others all have an exact matching pair. Can you find the one-off?

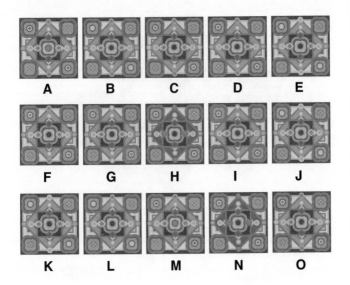

A B C D E

F G H I J

K L M N O

Answer on page 504

Plan View

Three of the patterns are a flat view of the picture below. Can you find the three that do not match?

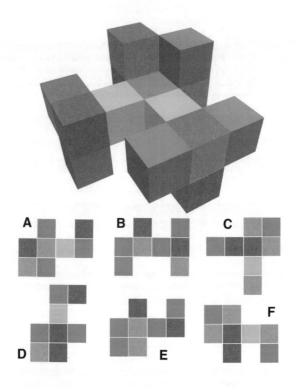

Answer on page 505

Scene It?

The four squares below can all be found in the picture grid – can you track them down? Beware, they may not be the right way up!

Answer on page 505

Shape Stacker

Can you work out the logic behind the numbers in these shapes, and the total of A x B x C?

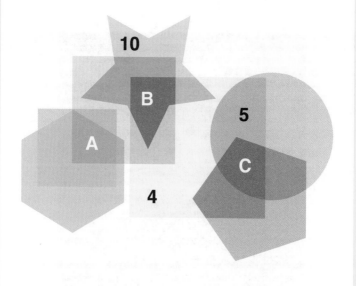

Answer on page 505

Silhouette

Which of the coloured-in pics matches our silhouette?

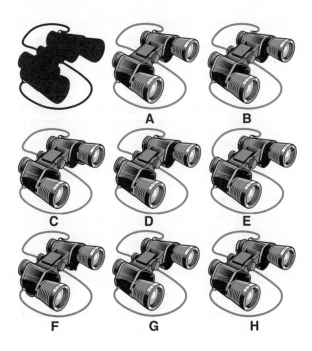

Answer on page 505

Sudoku

Complete the grid so that all rows and columns, and each outlined block of nine squares, contain the numbers 1, 2, 3, 4, 5, 6, 7, 8 and 9.

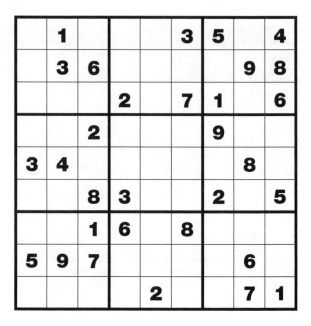

Answer on page 505

Sum People

Work out what number is represented by which person and replace the question mark.

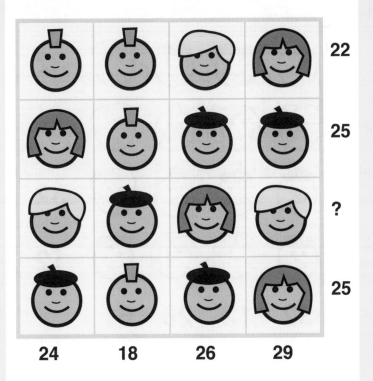

Answer on page 505

Sum People

Work out what number is represented by which person and replace
the question mark.

32 12 26 61

Answer on page 505

Weigh to Go

The coloured balls represent the numbers 2, 3, 4, 5 and 6. Can you work out which is which, and therefore how many green balls are required to balance the final scale?

Answer on page 505

Where's the Pair?

Only two of the shapes below are exactly the same – can you find the matching pair?

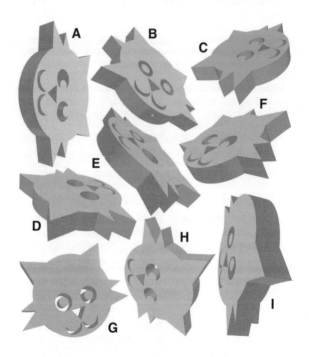

Answer on page 506

Same Difference

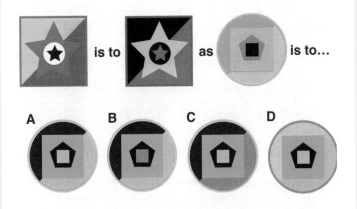

is to ... as ... is to...

A B C D

Answer on page 506

Scene It?

The four squares below can all be found in the picture grid – can you track down? Beware, they may not be the right way up!

Answer on page 506

Mirror Image

Only one of these pictures is an exact mirror image of the first one. Can you spot it?

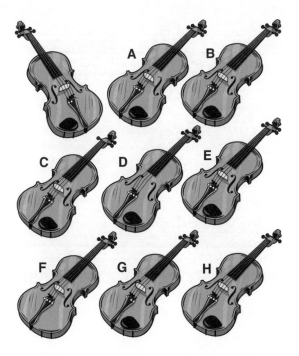

Answer on page 506

View from Above

Of the plan views below, only one of them is a true overhead representation of the scene shown here – can you work out which?

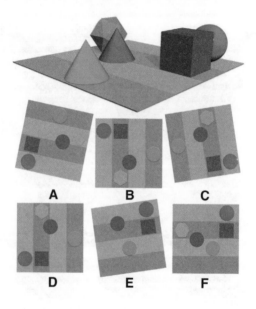

A   B   C

D   E   F

Answer on page 506

Can You Cut It?

Cut two straight lines through this shape to create three shapes that are identical.

Answer on page 506

Dice Maze

The colours on these dice represent a direction – up, down, left and right. Starting in the middle dce of the grid, follow the instructions correctly and you will visit every die in turn once only. What's the last die you visit on your trip?

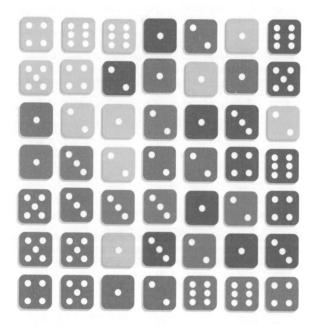

Answer on page 506

Dice Puzzle

Which of these dice is not like the other three?

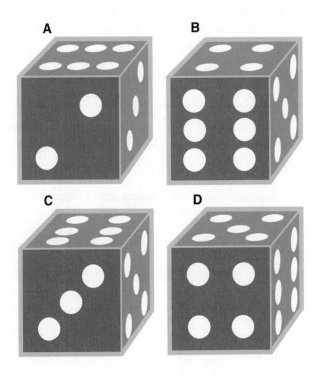

Answer on page 506

Floor Fillers

Below is a plan of a bathroom, showing the bath and other fixings, and next to it, some very oddly shaped pieces of marble. Can you arrange them to fill the floor?

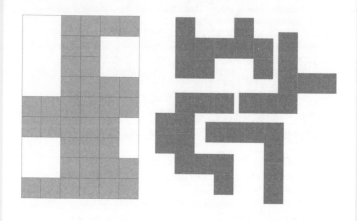

Answer on page 506

Hub Signs

What number should appear in the hub of the second wheel?

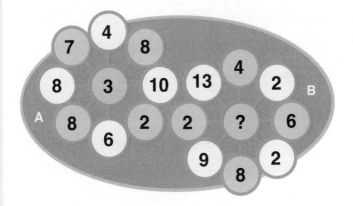

Answer on page 507

Jigsaw

Which four of the pieces below can complete the jigsaw and make a perfect square?

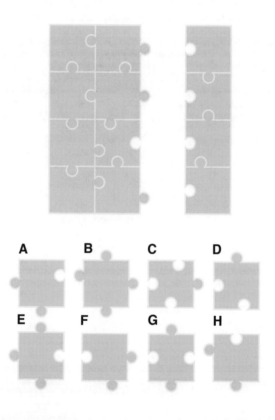

A B C D

E F G H

Answer on page 507

Latin Square

Complete the grid so that every row and column, and every outlined area, contains the letters A, B, C, D, E and F.

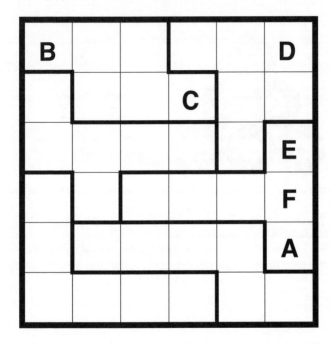

Answer on page 507

Logic Sequence

The balls below have been rearranged. Can you work out the new sequence of the balls from the clues given below?

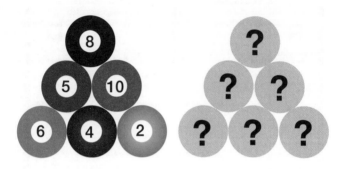

The top three balls total 22.
The 5 ball is immediately to the right of the 6, and isn't in contact with the 4 ball.
The 10 ball touches four others, but not the 6.

Answer on page 507

Minesweeper

The numbers in some squares in the grid indicate the exact number of black squares that should surround it. Shade these squares until all the numbers are surrounded by the correct number of black squares.

			2		0	2	
3	4	4					
1			2		3	4	
	1		1	3			2
1	2		3	4		3	
2					3	2	1
	4	5	5		3		
2		2			2	1	1

Answer on page 507

Pattern Pairs

Only one of the tiles below is unique; the other 14 all have an exact matching pair. Can you find the one-off?

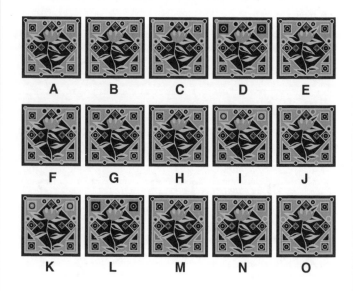

A   B   C   D   E

F   G   H   I   J

K   L   M   N   O

Answer on page 507

Shape Stacker

Can you work out the logic behind the numbers in these shapes, and the total of A + B?

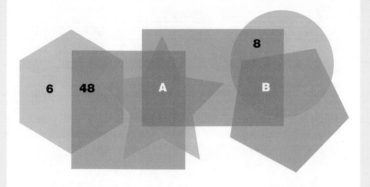

Answer on page 507

View from Above

Of the plan views below, only one of them is a true overhead representation of the scene shown here – can you work out which?

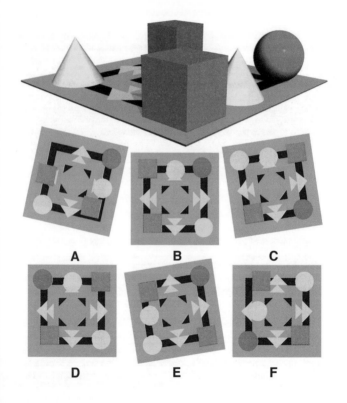

A

B

C

D

E

F

Answer on page 508

Battleships

The numbers on the side and bottom of the grid indicate occupied squares or groups of consecutive occupied squares in each row or column. Can finish the grid so that it contains three Cruisers, three Launches and three Buoys and the numbers tally?

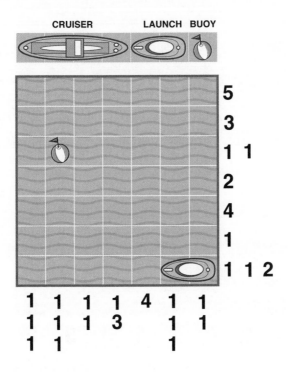

CRUISER LANGH BUOY

Camp Conifer

Every tree 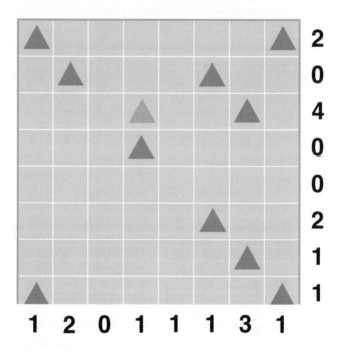 has one tent found horizontally or vertically adjacent to it. No tent can be in an adjacent square to another tent (even diagonally). The numbers by each row and column tell you how many tents are there. Can you locate all the tents?

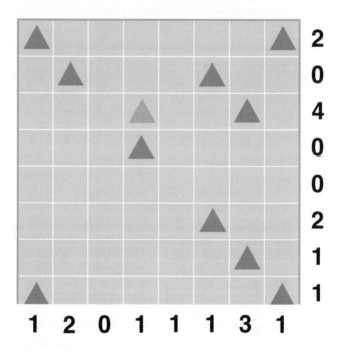

Answer on page 508

Patch of the Day

Place the shape over the grid so that no colour appears twice in the same row or column. Beware, the shape may not be the right way up!

Answer on page 508

Looplink

Connect adjacent dots with either horizontal or vertical lines to create a continuous unbroken loop which never crosses over itself. Some, but not all of the boxes are numbered. The numbers in these boxes tell you how many sides of that box are used by your unbroken line.

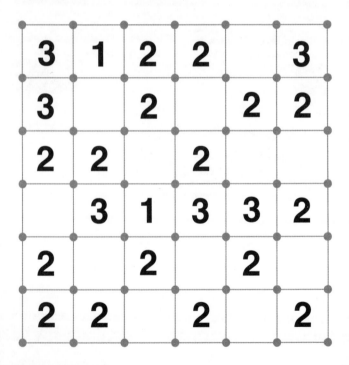

Answer on page 508

More or Less

The arrows indicate whether a number in a box is greater or smaller than an adjacent number. Complete the grid so that all rows and columns contain the numbers 1 to 6.

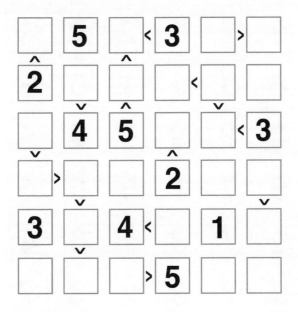

Answer on page 508

Number Chunks

Divide up the grid into four equal size, equally shaped parts, each containing numbers that add up to 40.

8	2	1	2	2	4
6	3	1	1	6	3
4	9	9	9	3	5
5	7	1	5	5	5
2	7	3	1	6	4
9	7	3	2	3	7

Answer on page 508

Safecracker

To open the safe, all the buttons must be pressed in the correct order before the "open" button is pressed. What is the first button pressed in your sequence?

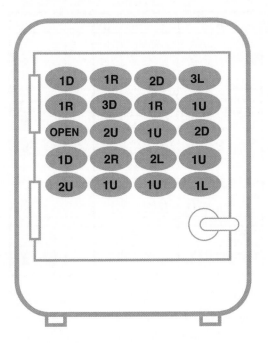

Answer on page 508

Sudoku

Complete the grid so that all rows and columns, and each outlined block of nine squares, contain the numbers 1, 2, 3, 4, 5, 6, 7, 8 and 9.

	2		1		8	3		
		7		2				5
4			7			1		
		1	4					8
	9					5		6
2			6	7				
7		6	8					3
8				9			2	
			3				6	4

Answer on page 509

Symbol Sums

These symbols represent the numbers 1 to 4. If the pink parrot represents the number 2, can you work out what the other parrots are representing and make a working sum?

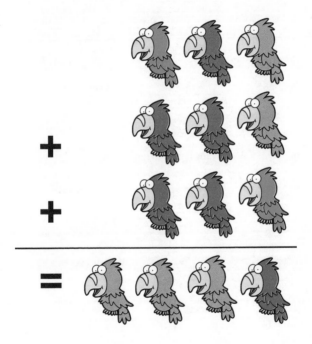

Answer on page 509

Where's the Pair?

Only two of these pictures are exactly the same. Can you spot the matching pair?

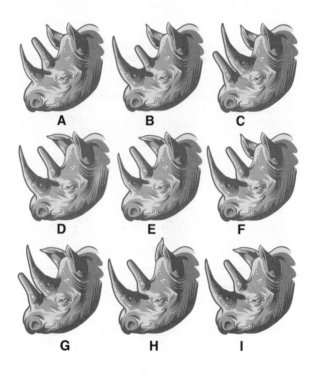

Answer on page 509

All Change

The colour of each square in pattern B is directly related to the colours in pattern A. The square colours in pattern C relate to pattern B the same way. Can you apply the same rules and fill in pattern D?

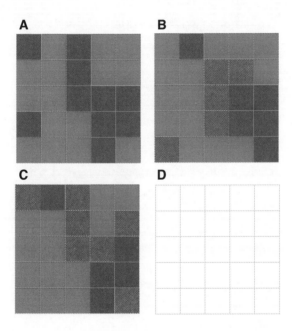

A

B

C

D

Answer on page 509

Battleships

The numbers on the side and bottom of the grid indicate occupied squares or groups of consecutive occupied squares in each row or column. Can you finish the grid so that it contains three Cruisers, four Launches and five Buoys and the numbers tally?

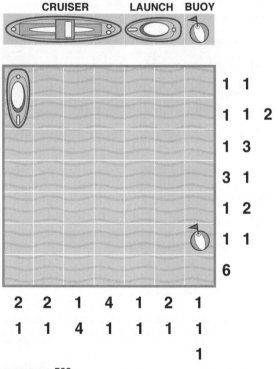

Answer on page 509

Camp Conifer

Evert tree 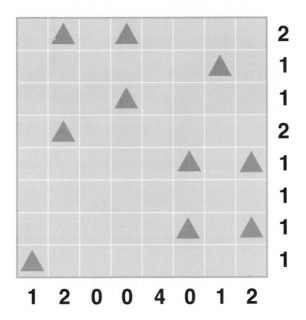 has one tent found horizontally or vertically adjacent to it. No tent can be in an adjacent square to another tent (even diagonally). The numbers by each row and column tell you how many tents are there. Can you locate all the tents?

Answer on page 509

Can You Cut It?

Cut two straight lines through this shape to create three shapes that are identical.

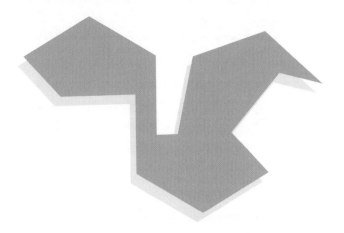

Answer on page 509

Chess

Can you place a queen, a bishop, a knight and a rook on this chessboard so that the red squares are attacked by exactly two pieces, the green one by 3 pieces and the yellow one by 4 pieces?

Answer on page 509

Five Point Problem

Discover the pattern behind the numbers on these pentagons and fill in the blanks to complete the puzzle.

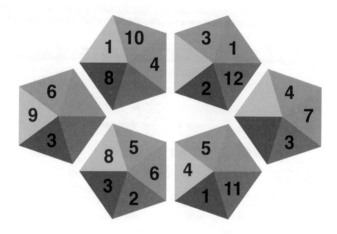

Answer on page 510

Gridlock

Which square correctly completes the grid?

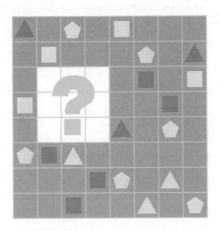

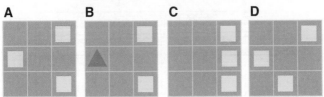

A   B   C   D

Answer on page 510

Killer Six

Complete the grid so that all rows and columns contain the numbers 1, 2, 3, 4, 5 and 6. Areas with a dotted outline contain numbers that add up to the total shown. Dotted boxes can contan the same number more than once, however.

9			7		10
16		6			
3		**6**	7	6	
	7			22	
12		11			4
				1	

Answer on page 510

Hub Signs

What number should appear in the hub of the second wheel?

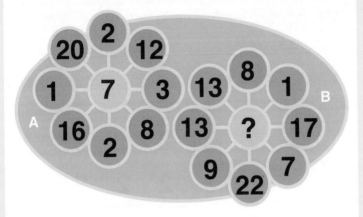

Answer on page 510

Looplink

Connect adjacent dots with either horizontal or vertical lines to create a continuous unbroken loop which never crosses over itself. Some, but not all of the boxes are numbered. The numbers in these boxes tell you how many sides of that box are used by your unbroken line.

1		2		2	2
2	2	3	2		3
	0	3	2	2	2
	3			2	
1		2	2	1	2
3	2	2	2		3

Answer on page 510

Magic Squares

Complete the square using nine consecutive numbers, so that all rows, columns and large diagonals add up to the same total.

Answer on page 510

The Great Divide

Divide up the grid into four equal size, equally shaped parts, each containing one each of the four different symbols.

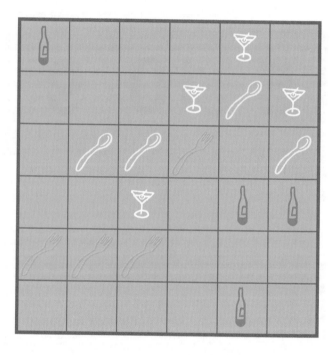

Answer on page 510

Percentage Point

Can you determine what percentage of this design is red? And what percentage of the blue squares in the design contain stars?

Answer on page 510

Scene It?

The four squares below can all be found in the picture grid – can you track them down? Beware, they may not be the right way up!

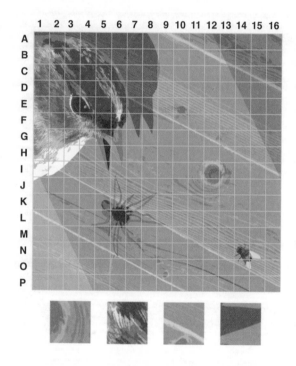

Answer on page 511

Small Logic

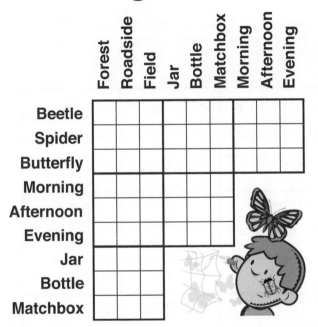

	Forest	Roadside	Field	Jar	Bottle	Matchbox	Morning	Afternoon	Evening
Beetle									
Spider									
Butterfly									
Morning									
Afternoon									
Evening									
Jar									
Bottle									
Matchbox									

Little Tom collects insects. Can you discover where he found these three, at what time of day, and what he put them in so he could take them home?

1) The spider was found in the evening, not in a field.
2) The butterfly was found in the forest, though not in the morning, and Tom didn't put it in a jar.
3) The creature found in a field was placed in a bottle.

Answer on page 511

Sudoku

Complete the grid so that all rows and columns, and each outlined block of nine squares, contain the numbers 1, 2, 3, 4, 5, 6, 7, 8 and 9.

		6		7		5	3	
8			1	3		2		
					2			
9				5			4	
		4			6		8	5
2	8		7	9		6		
	1			6				9
	7					4	2	1
5			4				6	

Answer on page 511

Think Back

Study these images for a minute, then cover them up and answer the five questions below.

Questions:
1. How many leaves has the yellow flower?
2. How many leaves in total have the flowers in red pots?
3. What colour is flower B?
4. Which flower has only the left leaf?
5. How many of the pink flowers have blue pots?

Answer on page 511

Sudoku

Fill in the numbers 1, 2, 3, 4, 5, 6, 7, 8, and 9 so they appear once only in each row, column and 9 x 9 grid

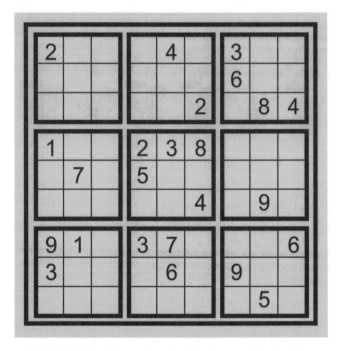

Answer on page 511

The Red Corner

Use the red corners to make the central number the same way in all three cases. What number should replace the question mark?

Answer on page 511

Chess

Can you place a queen, a bishop, a knight and a rook on this chessboard so that the red squares are attacked by exactly two pieces, the green ones by 3 pieces and the yellow one by 4 pieces?

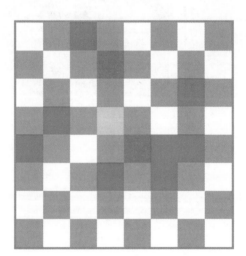

Answer on page 511

Sudoku Six

Complete the first grid so that every row and column contain all the letters ABJKY and Z. Do the same with grid 2 and the numbers 12345 and 6. To decode the finished grid, add the numbers in the shaded squares to the letters in the matching squares in the second (ie: A + 3 = D, Y + 4 = C) to get six new letters which can be arranged to spell the name of a famous composer.

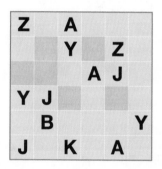

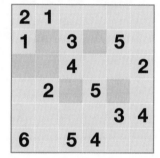

Answer on page 511

Cube Route

Can you crack the colour code and make your way from one green square to the other? Each colour represents up, down, left or right. The blue arrow tells you which way is up...

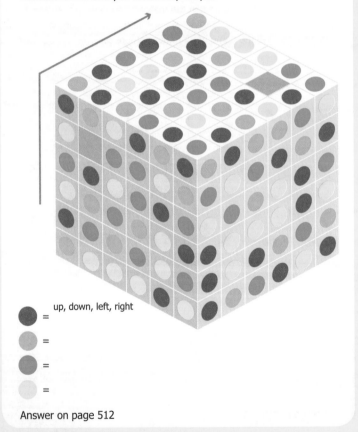

up, down, left, right

=

=

=

=

Answer on page 512

Pattern Pairs

Only one of the tiles below is unique; the others all have an exact matching pair. Can you find the one-off?

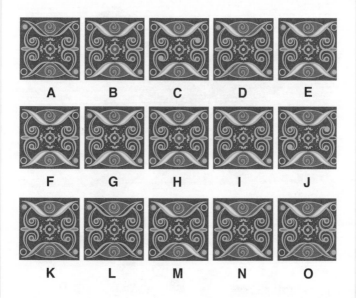

A   B   C   D   E

F   G   H   I   J

K   L   M   N   O

Answer on page 512

Plan View

Three of the patterns are a flat view of the picture below. Can you find the three that do not match?

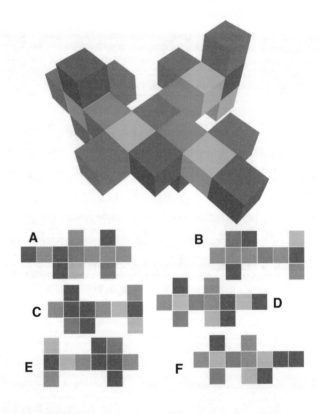

A

B

C

D

E

F

Answer on page 512

Number Mountain

Replace the question marks with numbers so that each pair of blocks adds up to the block directly above them.

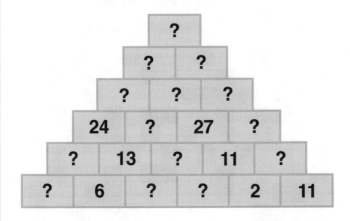

Answer on page 512

Symmetry

This picture, when finished, is symmetrical along a vertical line up the middle. Can you colour in the missing squares and work out what the picture is of?

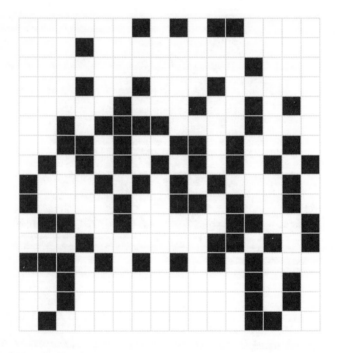

Answer on page 512

Scene It?

The four squares below can all be found in the picture grid – can you track them down? Beware, they may not be the right way up!

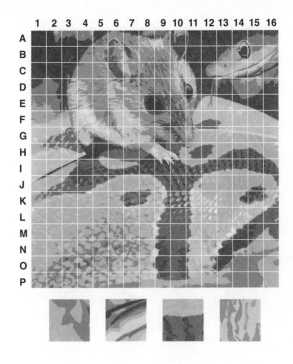

Answer on page 512

Cube Volume

These little cubes originally made a big cube measuring 15 cm x 15 cm x 15 cm. Now some of the little cubes have been removed, can you work out what volume the remaining cubes have now? Assume all hidden cubes are present.

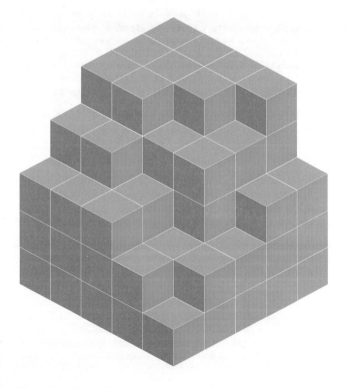

Answer on page 512

Dice Puzzle

Which of these dice is not like the other three?

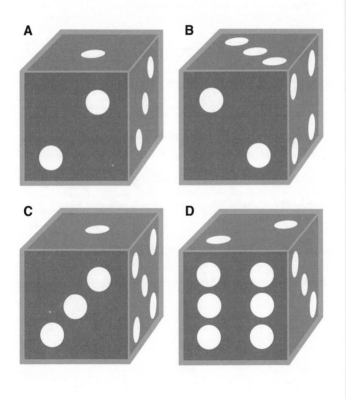

A

B

C

D

Answer on page 512

Five Star

Believe it or not, none of these stars is exactly alike. They represent every single combination of five colours - except one. Can you work out the colour placements on the missing star?

Answer on page 513

Killer Six

Complete the grid so that all rows and columns contain the numbers 1, 2, 3, 4, 5 and 6. Areas with a dotted outline contain numbers that add up to the total shown.

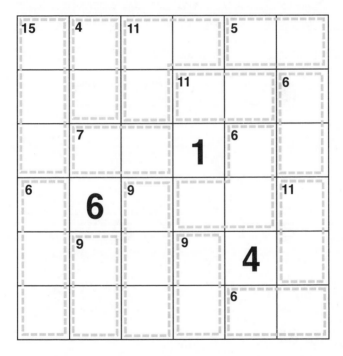

Answer on page 513

Masyu

Draw a single continuous line around the grid that passes through all the circles. The line must enter and leave each box in the centre of one of its four sides.
Black Circle: Turn left or right in the box, and the line must pass straight through the next and previous boxes. White Circle: Travel straight through the box, and the line must turn in the next and/or previous box.

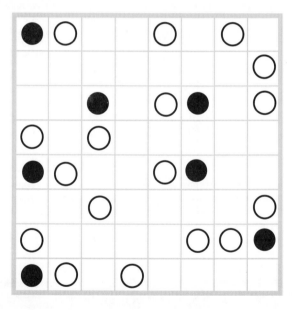

Answer on page 513

Mini Nonogram

The numbers by each row and column describe black squares and groups of black squares that are adjoining. Colour in all the black squares and a six number combination will be revealed.

					1					
		1			3	1	5			5
	3	5	5		5	1	5		1	1	5
1 1 1 1 1
1 1 1 1 1
3 3 1
1 1 1
1 1 1
1 3 3
1 1 1 1
1 1 1 1
1 1 1 1
1 3 1

Answer on page 513

Number Chunks

Divide up the grid into four equal size, equally shaped parts, each containing numbers that add up to 36.

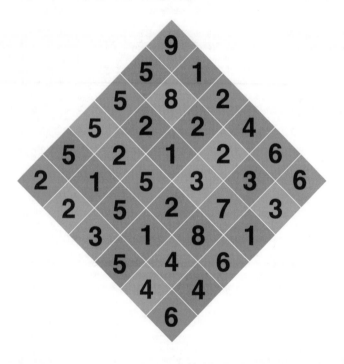

Answer on page 513

Floor Fillers

Below is a marked out floor waiting to be tiled, together with some pre-assembled groups of tiles... Can you fit them together so that they fill the floor?

Answer on page 513

Follow That

The sequence below follows a logical pattern. Can you work out which way the next pig in line faces, and what colour its tail is?

Answer on page 513

Jigsaw

Which four of the pieces below can complete the jigsaw and make a perfect square?

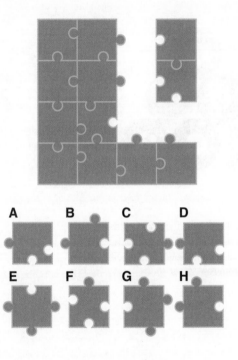

Answer on page 513

Logic Sequence

The balls below have been rearranged. Can you work out the new sequence of the balls from the clues given below?

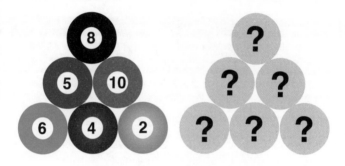

The 2 ball isn't touching the 5 or the 4.
The 4 ball is touching the 10 but not the 6.
The 8 ball is immediately to the left of the 6.
The bottom row totals 16.

Answer on page 514

Scales

The arms of these scales are divided into sections - a weight two sections away from the middle will be twice as heavy as a weight one section away. Can you arranged the supplied weights in such a way as to balance the whole scale?

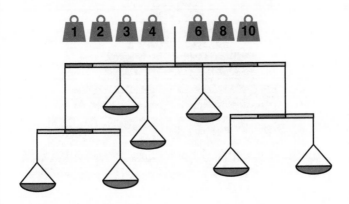

Answer on page 514

Number Mountain

Replace the question marks with numbers so that each pair of blocks adds up to the block directly above them.

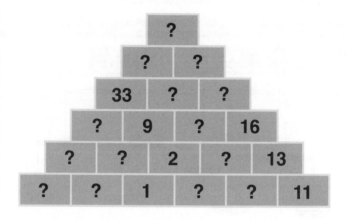

Answer on page 514

Knight's Move

Find an empty square in the grid that is one chess knight's move away from a blue, red and yellow circle. A knight's move is an 'L' shape – two squares sideways, up or down in any direction, followed by one square to the left or right.

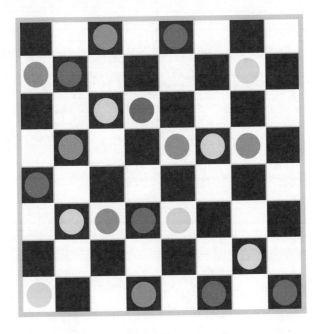

Answer on page 514

Weigh to Go

The coloured balls represent the numbers 3, 4, 5, 6 and 7. Can you work out which is which, and therefore how many red balls (unseen so far) are required to balance the final scale?

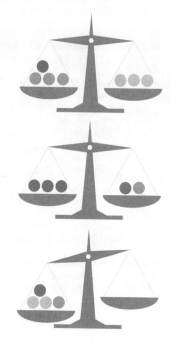

Answer on page 514

Mirror Image

Only one of these pictures is an exact mirror image of the first one. Can you spot it?

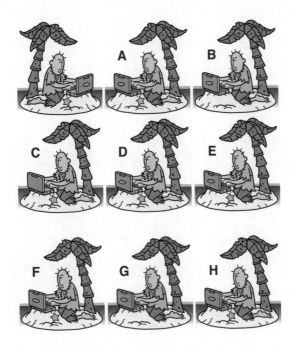

Answer on page 514

Silhouette

Which of the coloured-in pics matches our silhouette?

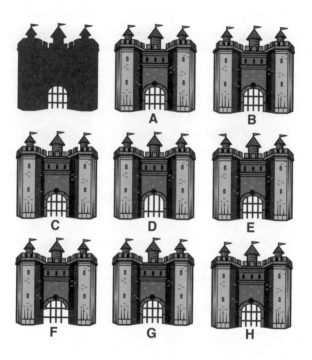

Answer on page 514

Symbol Sums

These symbols represent the numbers 1 to 4. Can you work out which colour knights are representing what numbers and make a working sum?

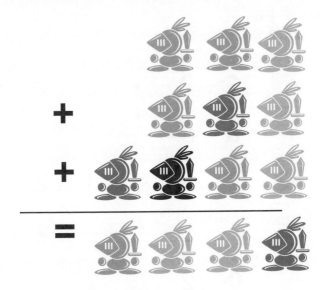

Answer on page 514

Looplink

Connect adjacent dots with either horizontal or vertical lines to create a continuous unbroken loop which never crosses over itself. Some, but not all of the boxes are numbered. The numbers in these boxes tell you how many sides of that box are used by your unbroken line.

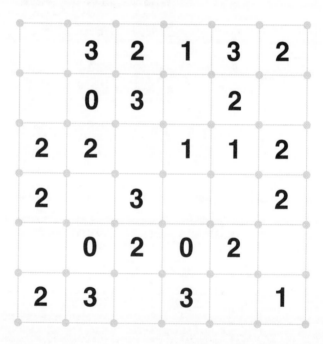

Answer on page 515

Sudoku

Complete the grid so that all rows and columns, and each outlined block of nine squares, contain the numbers 1, 2, 3, 4, 5, 6, 7, 8 and 9.

	8	1	2	3		5		4
3			4					8
	4	6			5			
	6			2		3		5
1		4						7
			7			9		
		3					8	
7	2			9		1		
			8		3	6		2

Answer on page 515

Matrix

Which of the four boxed figures completes the set?

Answer on page 515

Where's the Pair?

Only two of these pictures are exactly the same. Can you spot the matching pair?

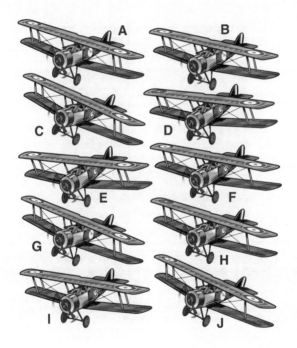

Answer on page 515

Gridlock

Which square correctly completes the grid?

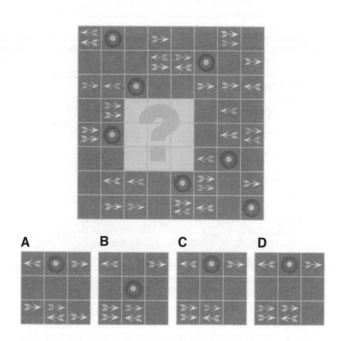

A   **B**   **C**   **D**

Answer on page 515

Think of a Number

Yellowbeard the pirate had 27 crew under him on his ship, the Blue Goose. He had less prisoners than that in the hold. One night, half of them escaped, leaving the ship exactly 15 percent less occupied than it was before. How many prisoners escaped?

Answer on page 515

Killer Sudoku

Complete the grid so that all rows and columns, and each outlined block of nine squares, contain the numbers 1, 2, 3, 4, 5, 6, 7, 8 and 9. Areas with a dotted outline contain numbers that add up to the total shown.

Answer on page 515

Think Back

Study these images for a minute, then cover them up and answer the five questions below.

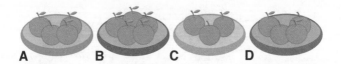

Question:
1. Which colour bowl contains only apples with leaves?
2. Which colour bowl has five apples?
3. How many apples has the bowl with three leaves?
4. How many apples have bowls A and C together?
5. How many apples in total are leafless?

Answer on page 515

Hub Signs

What number should appear in the hub of the second wheel?

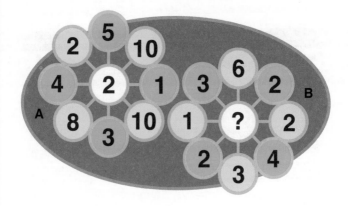

Answer on page 516

Small Logic

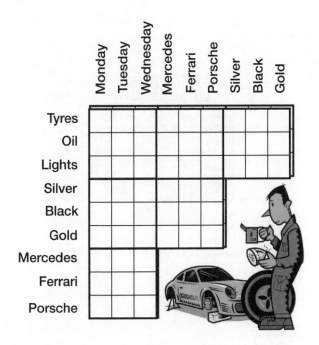

	Monday	Tuesday	Wednesday	Mercedes	Ferrari	Porsche	Silver	Black	Gold
Tyres									
Oil									
Lights									
Silver									
Black									
Gold									
Mercedes									
Ferrari									
Porsche									

Jack's garage has seen some fancy cars this week. From the clues below, can you work out when he worked on each car, what colour each was, and what jobs he had to do?

1) The Porsche was black, and didn't need an oil change
2) Jack changed tyres on Monday, but not on the Ferrari
3) The Ferrari was done before the lights but after the silver car

Answer on page 516

In the Area

Can you work out the approximate area that this tree is occupying, minus the oranges?

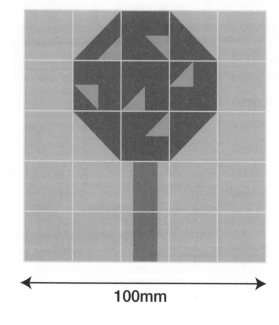

100mm

Answer on page 516

Symmetry

This picture, when finished, is symmetrical along a vertical line up the middle. Can you shade in the missing squares and work out what the picture is of?

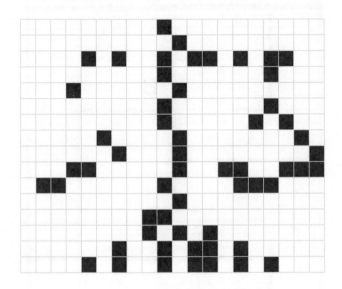

Answer on page 516

Latin Square

Complete the grid so that every row and column, and every outlined area, contains the letters A, B, C, D, E and F.

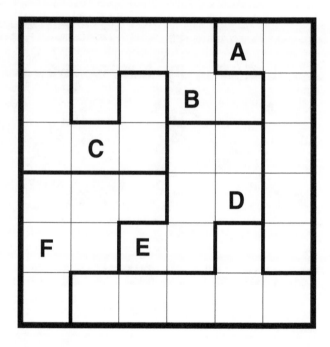

Answer on page 516

Percentage Point

Can you determine what percentage of the squares making up this design are not white, and do not contain any stars?

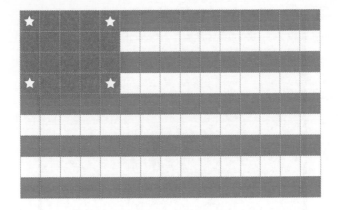

Answer on page 516

Magic Squares

Complete the square using nine consecutive numbers, so that all rows, columns and large diagonals add up to the same total.

Answer on page 516

Revolutions

Cog A has 8 teeth, cog B has 9, cog C has 10 and cog D has 18. How many revolutions must cog A turn through to get all the cogs into an upright position?

Answer on page 516

Treasure Island

The numbers on the side and bottom of the grid indicate occupied squares or groups of consecutive occupied squares in each row or column. Can you finish the grid so that it contains three of each item and the numbers tally?

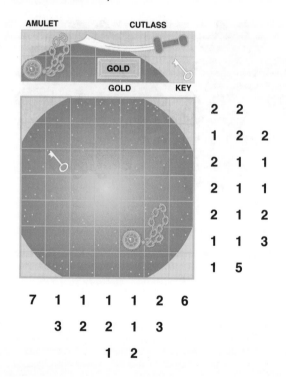

AMULET   CUTLASS

GOLD

GOLD   KEY

2	2			
1	2	2		
2	1	1		
2	1	1		
2	1	2		
1	1	3		
1	5			

7	1	1	1	1	2	6
	3	2	2	1	3	
			1	2		

Answer on page 517

Masyu

Draw a single continuous line around the grid that passes through all the circles. The line must enter and leave each box in the centre of one of its four sides.

Black Circle: Turn left or right in the box, and the line must pass straight through the next and previous boxes.

White Circle: Travel straight through the box, and the line must turn in the next and/or previous box.

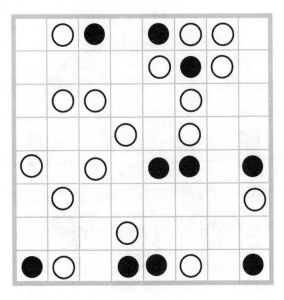

Answer on page 517

Roulette

The roulette ball is dropped into the wheel at the 0 section. When the ball falls into a number 15 seconds later, it has travelled at an average speed of 3 metres per second clockwise, while the wheel has travelled at an average 1 metre per second in the other direction. The ball starts rolling 50 centimetres away from the wheel's centre. Where does it land? Take pi as having a value of exactly 3.2.

Answer on page 517

Scene It?

The four squares below can all be found in the picture grid – can you track them drown? Beware, they may not be the right way up!

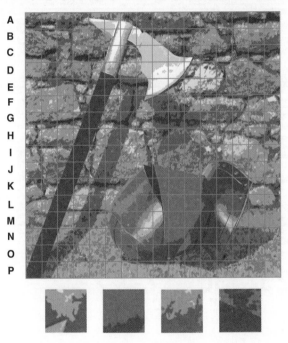

Answer on page 517

Sum People

Work out what number is represented by which person and replace the question mark.

Answer on page 517

Shuffle

Fill up the shuffle box so that each row, column and long diagonal contains a Jack, Queen, King and Ace of each suit.

Answer on page 517

The Red Corner

Use the red corners to make the central number the same way in all three cases. What number should replace the question mark?

Answer on page 517

Riddle

At the rocket scientists' canteen, two boffins were chatting in the queue. "How many kids do you have?" asked Professor Numero. "Three" replied Doctor Egghead. "Oh yeah? How old?," said Professor Numero. "Ah," said Dr Egghead, "Well, their ages add up to 13 and multiply to 36, and two of them are twins". "Hmm..." said the Professor. "My eldest is a girl," said Dr Egghead. "Aha! That makes all the difference," said Professor Numero, and promptly told the good Doctor the ages of all his children.

How did that last piece of information help, and how old are the Doctor's kids?

Answer on page 517

Sum People

Work out which number is represented by which person and fill in the question mark.

Answer on page 518

Spare Part

All these pictures below show constructions built from three units of the spare part. Except one! Can you find the dodgy design?

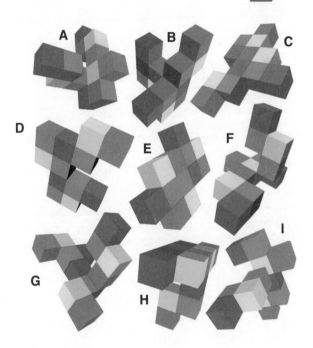

A B C

D

E F

G H I

Answer on page 518

Minesweeper

The numbers in some squares in the grid indicate the exact number of black squares that should surround it. Shade these squares until all the numbers are surrounded by the correct number of black squares.

	2	1	1		3		2
4		3		1			
			1			1	1
4		4		2		0	
	2	2			3	3	
2		2	4				
	3					6	3
2			3	4		3	

Answer on page 518

More or Less

The arrows indicate whether a number in a box is greater or smaller than an adjacent number. Complete the grid so that all rows and columns contain the numbers 1 to 6.

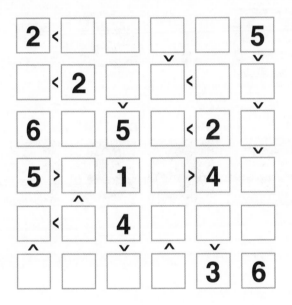

Answer on page 518

Next!

In the sequence below, which of the alternatives, A, B, C or D, should replace the question mark?

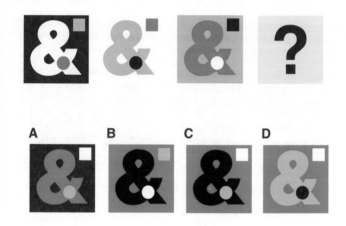

A   B   C   D

Answer on page 518

Patch of the Day

Place the patch over the grid so that no colour appears twice in the same row or column. Beware, the shape may not be the right way up!

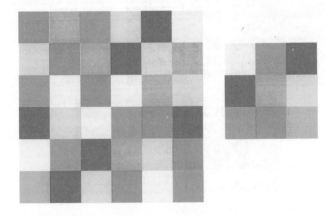

Answer on page 518

Signpost

Can you crack the logical secret behind the numbers by these footballers' names, and work out what number Fabregas might be?

Ronaldinho
252

Rooney
162

Messi
91

Crespo
24

Fabregas
?

Answer on page 518

Shape Stacker

Can you work out the logic behind the numbers in these shapes, and the total of A + B?

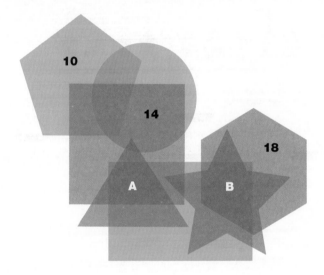

Answer on page 518

Scales

The arms of these scales are divided into sections – a weight two sections away from the middle will be twice as heavy as a weight one section away. Can you arranged the supplied weights in such a way as to balance the whole scale?

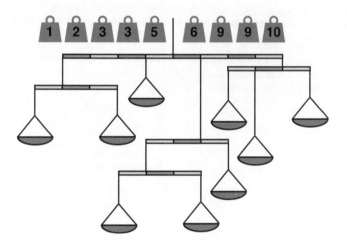

Answer on page 519

Safecracker

To open the safe, all the buttons must be pressed in the correct order before the "open" button is pressed. What is the first button pressed in your sequence?

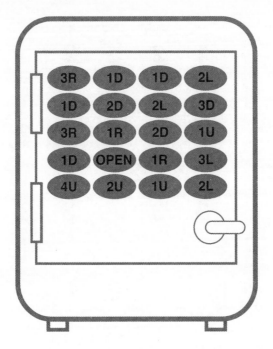

Answer on page 519

Radar

The numbers in some cells in the grid indicate the exact number of black cells that should border it. Shade these black, until all the numbers are surrounded by the correct number of black cells.

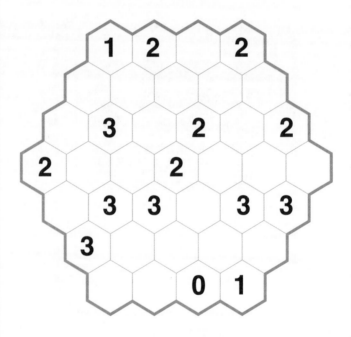

Answer on page 519

Pattern Pairs

Only one of the tiles below is unique; the other all have an exact matching pair. Can you find the one-off?

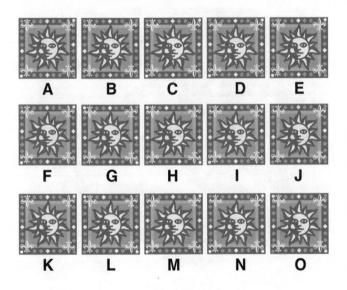

Answer on page 519

Odd One Out

Which of the shapes below is not the same as the other ones?

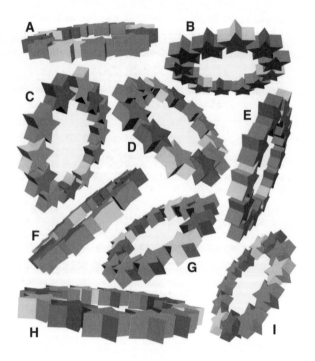

Answer on page 519

Plan View

Three of the patterns are a flat view of the picture below. Can you find the three that do not match?

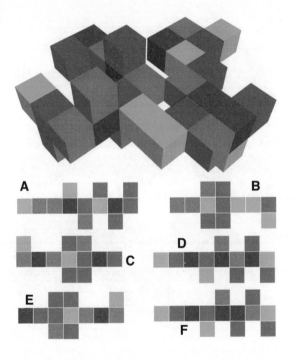

Answer on page 519

Where's the Pair?

Only two of the shapes below are exactly the same – can you find the matching pair?

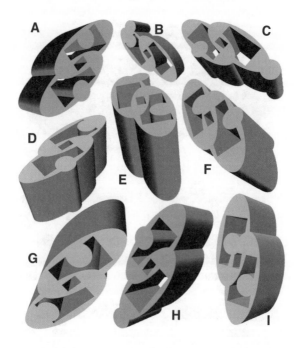

Answer on page 519

Answers

Page 350
Answer: B is the odd one out

Page 351
Answer: I

Page 352

Page 353

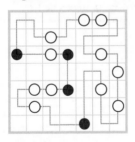

Page 354
Answer: B and G are the pair

Page 355
Solution: If its bordering cells are

predominantly blue, a cell becomes blue. If they are predominantly red, it becomes red. If the bordering cells are equal in number, the colour of a cell changes

Page 356

			▲					1
	▲	▲	▲					1
		▲			▲	▲		2
▲	▲	▲				▲		2
					▲	▲		1
▲	▲		▲		▲			2
					▲			1
		▲	▲					1

2 0 4 0 0 4 0 1

Page 357

C	M	W	B	I	U
I	C	M	U	B	W
B	U	I	C	W	M
U	I	B	W	M	C
W	B	U	M	C	I
M	W	C	I	U	B

6	1	2	3	5	4
3	6	4	5	1	2
5	4	1	6	2	3
4	5	3	2	6	1
2	3	5	1	4	6
1	2	6	4	3	5

M + 6 = S   U + 4 = Y
C + 1 = D   1 + 5 = N
B + 3 = E   W + 2 = Y

Answer: SYDNEY

Answers

Page 358
Answer: 6272 cubic centimetres. Each little cube measures 4 x 4 x 4 cm, or 64 cubic centimetres, and there are 98 little cubes left. 64 x 98 = 6272

Page 359

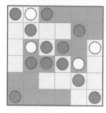

Page 360
Answer: B and F are the pair

Page 361

9	8	2	3	1	7	4	5	6
6	5	1	2	9	4	7	3	8
7	4	3	5	6	8	2	1	9
8	6	7	9	2	1	3	4	5
3	2	5	4	8	6	9	7	1
1	9	4	7	3	5	6	8	2
5	1	9	6	4	3	8	2	7
4	7	6	8	5	2	1	9	3
2	3	8	1	7	9	5	6	4

Page 362
Answer: L3, C13, O15, J5

Page 363
Answers:
1. 1
2. 1
3. 4
4. 3
5. Red

Page 364
Answer: M

Page 365
Answer: There are 25 honeycomb cells and 8 bees. Multiply both figures by 4 and we get an occupation percentage of 32%. 6 out of 8 bees, or three-quarters, or 75%, are awake.

Answers

Page 366

Page 367

Page 368

Answer: 12. The inner numbers are made up of the two outer numbers of the opposite segment multiplied.
4 x 3 = 12

Page 369

Solution: If its bordering triangles are predominantly black, a triangle becomes orange.

If they are predominantly orange, it becomes black.

If the bordering cells are equal in number, the triangle becomes yellow, and if the bordering triangles have now become predominantly yellow, it also becomes yellow

Page 370

Answer:
Blue = Right
Red = Left
Green = Up
Yellow = Down
The final die in your trip is the red 3, top of the fourth column.

Page 371

Solution: Each pentagon contains numbers that add up to 20, with the sides nearest adjoining pentagons adding up to 10

Page 372

Page 373

5	1	4	6	2	3
6	4	5	3	1	2
4	2	3	1	6	5
3	6	2	4	5	1
2	3	1	5	4	6
1	5	6	2	3	4

Answers

Page 374

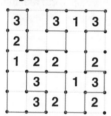

Page 375

Page 376

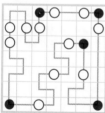

Page 377

Page 378
Answer: E

Page 379

3	1	5	2	4
1	2	4	5	3
4	5	3	1	2
2	3	1	4	5
5	4	2	3	1

Page 380
Answer: E is the odd one out

Page 381
Answer: E

Answers

Page 382
Answer: B, C & D are not views

Page 383
Answer: C10, J4, M11, H7

Page 384
Answer: 2520
The numbers represent the number of sides in the shape they occupy. When shapes overlap, the numbers are added together.

A: 6 + 4 + 4 = 14
B: 10 + 4 + 4 = 18
C: 5 + 4 + 1 = 10

14 x 18 x 10 = 2520

Page 385
Answer: D

Page 386

7	1	9	8	6	3	5	2	4
2	3	6	1	5	4	7	9	8
8	5	4	2	9	7	1	3	6
1	6	2	7	8	5	9	4	3
3	4	5	9	1	2	6	8	7
9	7	8	3	4	6	2	1	5
4	2	1	6	7	8	3	5	9
5	9	7	4	3	1	8	6	2
6	8	3	5	2	9	4	7	1

Page 387
Solution: 25

 4

 5

 6

 9

Page 388
Solution: 55

 1

 5

 10

 20

Page 389
Answer: Purple = 2, Red = 3, Yellow = 4, Green = 5, Blue = 6. Four green balls are required

Answers

Page 390
Answer: C and H are the pair.

Page 391
Answer: A

Page 392
Answer: B4, M7, F12, P11

Page 393
Answer: G

Page 394
Answer: C

Page 395

Page 396
Answer:
Blue = Right
Red = Left
Green = Up
Yellow = Down
The final die in your trip is the yellow 6, top of the third column

Page 397
Answer: D. The number six is turned 90 degrees compared to the other dice

Page 398

Answers

Page 399
Answer: 6. Subtract the numbers in the pink circles from the numbers in the yellow circles in both cases

Page 400
Answer: A, C, E and F

Page 401

B	F	E	A	C	D
F	A	D	C	E	B
D	C	A	B	F	E
A	E	C	D	B	F
C	B	F	E	D	A
E	D	B	F	A	C

Page 402

Page 403

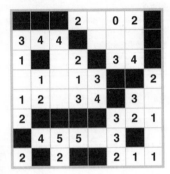

Page 404
Answer: J

Page 405
Answer: 720
Blue shapes have a value equal to the number of sides they have. Green shapes have a value of 2 x the number of sides they have. Where shapes overlap, their totals are multiplied.

(A) 8 x 8 x 10 = 640 +
(B) 10 x 8 x 1 = 80. Total 720

Answers

Page 406
Answer: D

Page 407

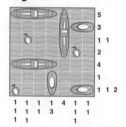

					5
					3
					1 1
					2
					4
					1
					1 1 2

1 1 1 1 4 1 1
1 1 1 3   1 1
1 1   1

Page 410

3	1	2	2	2		3
3		2		2	2	
2	2		2			
	3	1	3	3	2	
2		2		2		
2	2		2		2	

Page 408

▲	▲					▲	▲	2
	▲			▲				0
	▲			▲	▲	▲		4
		▲						0
								0
			▲	▲	▲			2
▲						▲		1
▲						▲	▲	1

1 2 0 1 1 1 3 1

Page 411

1	**5**	**2**‹	**3**	**6**›	**4**
2	**6**	**3**	**4**‹	**5**	**1**
6	**4**	**5**	**1**	**2**‹	**3**
5›	**3**	**1**	**2**	**4**	**6**
3	**2**	**4**‹	**6**	**1**	**5**
4	**1**	**6**›	**5**	**3**	**2**

Page 412

8	2	1	2	2	4
6	3	1	1	6	3
4	9	9	9	3	5
5	7	1	5	5	5
2	7	3	1	6	4
9	7	3	2	3	7

Page 409

Page 413

1D	1R	2D	3L
1R	3D	1R	1U
OPEN	2U	1U	2D
1D	2R	2L	1U
2U	1U	1U	1L

Answers

Page 414

5	2	9	1	6	8	3	4	7
1	3	7	9	2	4	6	8	5
4	6	8	7	3	5	1	9	2
6	7	1	4	5	9	2	3	8
3	9	4	2	8	1	5	7	6
2	8	5	6	7	3	4	1	9
7	1	6	8	4	2	9	5	3
8	4	3	5	9	6	7	2	1
9	5	2	3	1	7	8	6	4

Page 415
Answer: green 1, pink 2, purple 3, red 4

Page 416
Answer: D and I are the pair

Page 417

Solution: If its bordering squares (not diagonals) are predominantly red, a square becomes red. If they are predominantly blue it becomes blue. If the bordering cell colours are equal in number, the square becomes grey and if the bordering squares have now become predominantly grey, a square also becomes grey.

Page 418

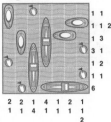

Page 419

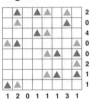

Page 420

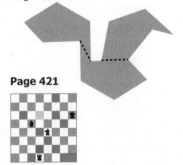

Page 421

509

Answers

Page 422

Solution: Each pentagon contains numbers that add up to 24, with the sides facing each other on adjoining pentagons, when multiplied together, also making 24

Page 423

Answer: A. Each row and column in the grid contains shapes whose sides total 12, two of which are yellow and one of which is red

Page 424

3	1	4	5	2	6
5	6	1	2	3	4
1	5	6	3	4	2
2	4	3	1	6	5
4	3	2	6	5	1
6	2	5	4	1	3

Page 425

Answer: 2. Divide the total of the numbers in the blue circles by the total of the numbers in the green circles in each case

Page 426

1		2		2	2
2	2	3	2		3
	0	3	2	2	2
	3			2	
1		2	2	1	2
3	2	2	2		3

Page 427

5	10	9
12	8	4
7	6	11

Page 428

Page 429

Answer: There are 38 red squares in the design, which is made up of 100 squares, so 38% of the design is red. There are 24 blue squares, 6 of which have stars on them, so one quarter, or 25% of the blue squares contain stars

Answers

Page 430
Answer: J12, B2, P9, F7

Page 431

	Forest	Roadside	Field	Jar	Bottle	Matchbox	Morning	Afternoon	Evening
Beetle	O	O	X	O	X	O	X	O	O
Spider	X	O	O	O	O	O	O	X	O
Butterfly	X	O	O	O	O	X	O	X	O
Morning	O	O	X	O	X	O			
Afternoon	X	O	O	O	O	O			
Evening	O	X	O	O	O	O			
Jar	O	X	O						
Bottle	O	O	X						
Matchbox	X	O	O						

Page 432

1	2	6	9	7	8	5	3	4
8	4	7	1	3	5	2	9	6
3	5	9	6	4	2	1	7	8
9	6	1	8	5	3	7	4	2
7	3	4	2	1	6	9	8	5
2	8	5	7	9	4	6	1	3
4	1	2	3	6	7	8	5	9
6	7	3	5	8	9	4	2	1
5	9	8	4	2	1	3	6	7

Page 433
Answer:
1. 2
2. 2
3. Pink
4. E
5. 2

Page 434

2	8	9	6	4	7	3	1	5
4	5	7	1	8	3	6	2	9
6	3	1	9	5	2	7	8	4
1	9	4	2	3	8	5	6	7
8	7	2	5	9	6	4	3	1
5	6	3	7	1	4	8	9	2
9	1	8	3	7	5	2	4	6
3	2	4	4	6	1	9	7	8
7	4	6	8	2	9	1	5	3

Page 435
Answer: 36. Add all the red corners and multiply the total by two. 3 + 3 + 7 + 5 = 18 x 2 = 36

Page 436

Page 437
B+6=H Z+1=A K+3=N Y+5=D A+4=E J+2=L

Solution: HANDEL

Z	K	A	B	Y	J
B	A	Y	J	Z	K
K	Y	B	A	J	Z
Y	J	Z	K	B	A
A	B	J	Z	K	Y
J	Z	K	Y	A	B

2	1	6	4	3	5
1	4	3	2	5	6
3	5	4	6	1	2
4	2	1	5	6	3
5	6	2	1	3	4
6	3	5	4	1	2

Answers

Page 438

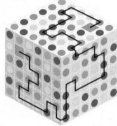

 = up

= left

= down

= right

Page 439
Answer: N

Page 440
Answer: A, E & F are not views.

Page 441

		216			
	109	107			
	53	56	51		
24	29	27	24		
11	13	16	11	13	
5	6	7	9	2	11

Page 442

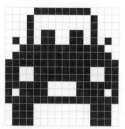

Page 443
Answer: O2, C15, H14, E6

Page 444
Answer: 2484 cubic centimetres. Each little cube measures 3 x 3 x 3 cm, or 27 cubic centimetres, and there are 92 little cubes left. 27 x 92 = 2484

Page 445
Answer: B. The right hand side should be showing a six

Answers

Page 446

Page 447

5	1	6	4	2	3
4	3	1	5	6	2
6	2	5	1	3	4
3	6	4	2	1	5
1	5	2	3	4	6
2	4	3	6	5	1

Page 448

Page 449

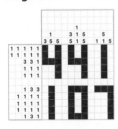

Page 450

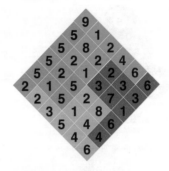

Page 451

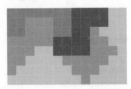

Page 452
Answer: Facing left with a pink tail. Two pigs with the same coloured tail are followed by a left-facing pig. Two pigs facing the same way are followed by one with a pink tail

Page 453
Answer: A, C, E and H

Answers

Page 454

Page 455

Page 456

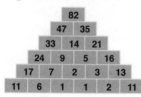

Page 457

Page 458

Answer: Purple = 3, Green = 4,
Blue = 5, Yellow = 6, Red = 7.
Three red balls are required

Page 459
Answer: D

Page 460
Answer: H

Page 461
Answer:
Orange 1
Black 2
Blue 3
Green 4

Answers

Page 462

2	3	2	1	3	2
3	0	3	1	2	2
2	2	2	1	1	2
2	2	3	3	3	2
3	0	2	0	2	2
2	3	3	3	2	1

Page 463

9	8	1	2	3	7	5	6	4
3	7	5	4	6	1	2	9	8
2	4	6	9	8	5	7	3	1
8	6	7	1	2	9	3	4	5
1	9	4	3	5	6	8	2	7
5	3	2	7	4	8	9	1	6
6	1	3	5	7	2	4	8	9
7	2	8	6	9	4	1	5	3
4	5	9	8	1	3	6	7	2

Page 464

 Every vertical and horizontal line contains one purple, one yellow and one white outer box. Each line also contains one purple inner diamond and two yellow ones. Finally each line contains one purple star and two yellow ones. The missing image should be a yellow outer box with a purple inner diamond and a yellow star

Page 465

Answer: B and G are the pair

Page 466

Solution: C. Each row and column in the grid contains a target, two gold arrows (one pointing left and one right) and three blue arrows (two of which point right and one left)

Page 467

Solution: 6. There were 12 prisoners in the hold before the escape, making 40 people in all on the ship, and 15 percent of 40 is 6

Page 468

2	9	3	5	1	8	4	6	7
8	4	5	3	6	7	2	9	1
1	7	6	9	4	2	3	5	8
4	6	2	7	8	9	1	3	5
3	1	9	2	5	6	8	7	4
5	8	7	4	3	1	6	2	9
6	3	1	8	7	5	9	4	2
9	5	4	1	2	3	7	8	6
7	2	8	6	9	4	5	1	3

Page 469

Answers:
1. Blue
2. Blue
3. 4
4. 7
5. 4

Answers

Page 470

Answer: 4. Multiply all the numbers in pink circles and add all the numbers in green circles. Divide the pink total by the green one.

$3 \times 2 \times 4 \times 2 = 48$

$1 + 6 + 2 + 3 = 12$

48 divided by 12 is 4

Page 471

	Monday	Tuesday	Wednesday	Mercedes	Ferrari	Porsche	Silver	Black	Gold
Tyres	X	O	O	X	O	O	X	O	O
Oil	O	X	O	O	X	O	O	O	X
Lights	O	O	X	O	O	X	O	X	O
Silver	X	O	O	X	O	O			
Black	O	O	X	O	X	O			
Gold	O	X	O	O	O	X			
Mercedes	X	O	O						
Ferrari	O	X	O						
Porsche	O	O	X						

Page 472

Answer: 2550 square millimetres. Each 20 x 20 square represents 400 mm². 4 squares, 4 half-square triangles and 2 half-squares make up the tree. Minus 250mm² that make up the oranges

Page 473

Page 474

B	F	C	D	A	E
D	A	F	B	E	C
E	C	A	F	B	D
A	E	B	C	D	F
F	D	E	A	C	B
C	B	D	E	F	A

Page 475

Answer: There are 135 squares in the design. 50 are white and 4 contain stars. 135 divided by 54 is 2.5. 100 divided by 2.5 is 40, so 54 represents 40% of 135. The squares that are not white and do not contain stars must therefore represent the other 60%

Page 476

10	9	14
15	11	7
8	13	12

Page 477

Answer: 22 and a half revolutions of cog A, which will make exactly 20 revolutions of cog B, 18 revolutions of cog C and 10 revolutions of cog D

Answers

Page 478

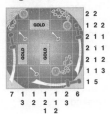

```
              2 2
          1 2 2
          2 1 1
          2 i 1
          2 1 2
          1 1 3
          1 5
7 1 1 1 1 2 6
  3 2 2 1 3
        1 2
```

Page 479

Page 480

Answer: In the number 6 space. The ball travels at a speed of 4 metres per second (relative to the wheel) for 15 seconds, making a distance of 6000 centimetres in a clockwise direction. The circumference of the wheel is 320 centimetres (2 x pi (3.2) x radius (50cm)). The ball must then travel 18.75 laps of the wheel, placing it three quarters of the way around the wheel in a clockwise direction, in the 6 space

Page 481

Answer: F8, N10, B16, O2

Page 482

Solution: 27

 2

 4

 6

 13

Page 483

Page 484

Answer: 50. Multiply the two largest red corners, then multiply the two smallest corners. Subtract the smaller total from the larger. $8 \times 7 = 56$. $6 \times 1 = 6$. $56 - 6 = 50$

Page 485

Answer: 9, 2 and 2. Before he knew that the twins were younger than the single child, the Professor could have come up with the answer 6, 6 and 1

Answers

Page 486

Answer: 18

 3

 1

 5

 11

Page 487

Answer: B

Page 488

Page 489

2‹	6	3	4	1	5
1‹	2	6	3‹	5	4
6	4	5	1‹	2	3
5›	3	1	6›	4	2
3‹	5	4	2	6	1
4	1	2	5	3	6

Page 490

Answer: C. With each new image, the dot takes the colour of the previous box, the square takes the colour of the previous dot, the ampersand takes the colour of the previous square, and the box takes the colour of the previous ampersand

Page 491

Page 492

Answer: 66. Score one for a consonant and two for a vowel, then multiply the total by the alphabetical position of the first letter. $5 + 6 = 11$, $11 \times 6 = 66$

Page 493

Answer: 85. Pink shapes have a value equal to twice the number of sides they have. Blue shapes have a value of 3 x the number of sides they have. Where shapes overlap, their totals are added together. (A) $8 + 9 + 12 = 29 +$ (B) $8 + 18 + 30 = 56$. Total 85

Answers

Page 494

Page 495

Page 496

Page 497
Answer: N

Page 498
Answer: F is the odd one out

Page 499
Answer: B, C and F are not views

Page 500
Answer: C and H are the pair

Your puzzle notes

Your puzzle notes

Your puzzle notes

Your puzzle notes

Your puzzle notes

Your puzzle notes

Your puzzle notes

Your puzzle notes

Your puzzle notes